Should Current Generations Make Reparation for Slavery?

Political Theory Today

Janna Thompson, *Should Current Generations Make Reparation for Slavery?*

Janna Thompson

Should Current Generations Make Reparation for Slavery?

polity

First published in 2018 by Polity Press

Polity Press
65 Bridge Street
Cambridge CB2 1UR, UK

Polity Press
101 Station Landing
Suite 300
Medford, MA 02155, USA

ISBN-13: 978-1-5095-1641-4
ISBN-13: 978-1-5095-1642-1(pb)

A catalogue record for this book is available from the British Library.

Typeset in 11 on 15 Sabon by Servis Filmsetting Ltd, Stockport, Cheshire
Printed and bound in the United Kingdom by Clays Ltd, St Ives PLC

For further information on Polity, visit our website: politybooks.com

Contents

Preface

The British Parliament banned the slave trade in 1807 and abolished slavery in the British Empire in 1833. France abolished slavery in its colonies in 1848, and slavery in America officially ended in 1865. But its legacy remains. Slavery profoundly affected the modern world. It brought prosperity to European countries and the United States. It devastated many African communities and reduced others to dependency, sowing the seeds that later led to the European colonisation of Africa. It produced racially divided nations scarred by a history of prejudice, discrimination, distrust and fear. It fuels conflicts about history and national identity. Generation after generation of citizens have inherited the effects of slavery and its aftermath. 'The past is never dead', as William Faulkner once wrote. 'It's not even past.'

What should we do about the legacy of slavery? An answer gaining currency in recent years is that citizens of former slave-trading or slave-owning societies and beneficiaries of slavery should make reparation to the descendants of slaves and to communities that have been harmed by slavery and the slave trade. The World Conference Against Racism (2001) ruled that reparation to Africa for the slave trade and colonialism should at least be a topic for discussion. Heads of governments in the Caribbean established a commission in 2013 to mount a moral and legal case for reparation for slavery and other injustices of former colonial powers. The National Coalition of Blacks for Reparation in America (N'COBRA) has been campaigning for reparation for slavery since 1987.

Demands for reparation are dismissed by most European and American leaders and rejected by many citizens. Why should present people take responsibility for a wrong that happened so long ago? How can descendants of slaves be entitled to reparation for slavery? And how do we determine how much (if anything) is owed?

Should current generations make reparation for slavery? The answer in this book is 'yes they should'. But a case for reparation invites a critical response. Do *you* think that current generations owe reparation for slavery? Read this book and make your judgement.

1

Slavery and Reparation

Slavery is morally wrong. Every moral theory of modern philosophy condemns it.[1] To enslave people is to violate their basic human rights. Treating people as property that can be bought and sold and used as their owner pleases offends against what the eighteenth-century philosopher, Immanuel Kant, regarded as the bedrock of morality: that people should be treated as ends and not merely as means. Slavery denies people ownership over their own bodies, a natural right that Locke, the influential

[1] There is one possible exception to the statement that no modern moral theory condones slavery. Utilitarianism, the view that we should act to maximise well-being, seems capable in theory of endorsing slavery if the well-being produced by a slave society outweighs the misery of slaves. R.M. Hare discusses this possibility in 'What is Wrong with Slavery?' (1979) and concludes that the harmful consequences likely to result from any system of slavery are sufficient to show that a utilitarian should condemn slavery.

seventeenth-century political philosopher, took to be the foundation of a just society. Slavery, as it was commonly practised, broke up families and tore children away from their parents. It inflicted terror, misery and pain on millions of men and women who were abducted from their communities and shackled into slave ships. Those who survived the cramped and unhealthy conditions of the voyage were forced to work often under brutal conditions and were beaten, raped and sometimes worked to death by their owners.

Slavery is an ancient institution and it continues to exist in some places in the world. In the eighteenth and nineteenth centuries it became a major source of wealth for Europeans who exploited and colonised the New World. Following the Arabs, who had been slave traders since medieval times, the Portuguese and Spanish enslaved Africans and used them to produce crops of coffee, tobacco and sugar for European markets. The Dutch, British and French soon joined them. In the American colonies slaves became an important source of labour, particularly in the South, where tobacco and later cotton growing became the major source of revenue. To supply an ever-increasing demand for slaves, a lucrative trade took Africans by the shipload from forts along the West African coast to colonies in the Americas and the islands of the Caribbean. Filled with the products of slave labour the ships sailed to ports in Europe and returned to Africa with cotton cloth from Manchester factories, linens from France and other products to sell to African chiefs in exchange for more slaves.

Great Britain soon became a dominant participant in this trade. In the ten years from 1721 to 1730 the British carried well over 100,000 slaves to Barbados, Jamaica and North America. The number increased in the following years and the prosperity of Liverpool, the major British slave port, and Manchester, the supplier of cotton goods, came to depend heavily on the slave trade. At the height of the slave trade in the 1780s more than 70,000 Africans were shipped to ports along the coastlines of North and South America and the Caribbean every year. Half of that number were carried by British ships. Trade depending on slaves was responsible for an estimated four fifths of the income that Britain extracted from its New World colonies.[2]

Britain prospered from slavery and the slave trade, and so did other European countries. The

[2] For information about the slave trade and slavery in the New World and their economic effects see Dunn (1972) and Thomas (1997).

revenues from the coffee and sugar plantations of Saint-Domingue (later Haiti) made France wealthy and powerful. Producing this wealth required a continual supply of slaves. An estimated 685,000 slaves were brought into Saint-Domingue during the eighteenth century alone. Life for a slave working in the coffee or cane fields of that island was brutal, nasty and often short. On average half of the slaves who arrived from Africa died within a few years.

In the United States before the Civil War – the conflict between North and South in 1861–5 that ended slavery – cotton grown by slaves produced over half of the nation's export earnings and per capita income in the southern states was one of the highest in the world. Almost 4 million slaves were working on southern plantations by the advent of the War.

Challenging Slavery

Slavery not only benefited captains of slave ships and plantation owners, but also shareholders of businesses that depended on slavery, workers in trades that supported it and consumers of cheap cotton goods. They were not inclined to question its morality. Defenders claimed that slaves were better off labouring in Christian countries than living in the barbaric, heathen societies of Africa. But opposition to slavery, inspired by religion or ideas about rights, had existed in European culture since the Middle Ages. Quakers campaigned against slavery during the eighteenth century and gradually won over public opinion in northern America and Great Britain. Enlightenment philosophers, who thought that reason rather than religion or conventional opinion was the basis for morality, were discomforted by the incompatibility between the institution of slavery and their belief in the natural rights of all human beings.

Inspired by the ideals of the French Revolution in 1789, slaves in Saint-Domingue rose up in 1791 and demanded the rights of man and citizen proclaimed by French revolutionaries. After defeating an army sent by the then ruler of France, Napoleon, in 1802, they created the independent nation of Haiti. As a price for recognising Haiti as an independent country France demanded 150 million gold francs as reparation to slave owners who had lost their property – ten times Haiti's annual revenue at that time. To pay this crippling debt the new country had no choice but to borrow from French banks that charged exorbitant rates of interest. Haiti was still paying reparations to France until 1947.[3]

Through the last decades of the eighteenth century opposition to slavery grew. After a long struggle, abolitionists in Britain prevailed and Parliament banned the slave trade in 1807. Most other countries, including France in 1817 and the United States in 1808, supported the ban on the slave trade, but slave traders continued to operate and slave owners, especially in the American South, could rely on the natural increase of slaves to maintain their supply. Slavery did not come to an end in the United States until President Lincoln's Emancipation Proclamation in 1865.

Reparative Demands

Shortly after the end of America's Civil War, Thaddeus Stevens, a US Congressman who had been an opponent of slavery, proposed that reparation be made to former slaves in the form of land confiscated from former slave owners and support-

[3] British slave owners also got compensation from the government when it banned slavery in 1833. Information about slavery in Saint-Domingue and the Haitian revolution is in Dubois (2004).

ers of slavery, along with payments to enable former slaves to establish themselves as independent farmers (Salzberger and Tuck 2004: 64–5). His bill was voted down and most of the land confiscated during the War was returned to its former owners. Most freed slaves had little choice but to return to their plantations or to accept positions as tenant farmers and subordination to white landlords.

Some Americans continued to call for reparation, but the unwillingness of the federal and state governments to consider grants or payments to former slaves and their descendants put it out of reach. The 1988 decision of the federal government to pay reparation to Japanese-Americans who were interned during World War II set a precedent that revived the movement for reparation for slavery (Henry 2003). The houses of the American Congress passed resolutions of apology for slavery in 2008 and 2009 but refused to pay reparation. No United States president has made an official apology. No reparation has ever been offered to descendants of slaves.

Elsewhere in the world acknowledgement of the wrong of slavery became a common way of addressing this historical injustice. Jacques Chirac, when president of France, instituted a national day of commemoration in 2006 to remember the stain of slavery in the country's history. François Hollande, during a presidential visit to the Caribbean in 2015, acknowledged a debt to Haiti but insisted it was moral and not financial. Tony Blair, when British prime minister, expressed deep sorrow in 2006 for Britain's role in the slave trade but offered no apology or financial reparations. David Cameron, during his 2015 visit to Jamaica as British prime minister, said that making an apology and paying reparation for slavery was not the right approach.

What is Reparation?

The ancient Greek philosopher Aristotle laid down the basics of reparative justice in the *Nicomachean Ethics*. If a wrong has been done, if someone unjustly takes something from another, then the wrongdoer is required to divest himself of his unjust gain so that it can be restored to the victim of the wrong.

His account embodies three principles of reparative justice. The first requires perpetrators to return what they have unjustly taken from their victims. If someone steals your bicycle then she should give it back. If she has lost it, then she owes you compensation equal to its value. The second principle prohibits anyone from benefiting from an injustice. Perpetrators must be forced to surrender the gains they have made from a wrong. And the third requires that victims should be compensated so that the harm caused by the injustice is removed. Together these principles express the guiding idea of reparation: that injustice creates an imbalance in the moral order that must be set right. Justice is accomplished when all those affected are returned to the situation they were in before the injustice took place – so far as this is possible.

The first principle focuses on restitution of stolen property, the second on the divestment of unjust gains that result from a wrong, and the third on the entitlement of the victim to compensation for harm. In Aristotle's account, all three are satisfied when the perpetrator is forced to return what he has wrongfully taken to the person from whom it was taken. However, the principles can operate independently. The first principle requires the return of stolen property even when the victim was not harmed by its absence. The second principle can require a person to surrender unjust gains even when there is no longer a victim to whom a return can be made. Nor does the prohibition against benefiting from an injustice apply only to wrongdoers. A person who unwittingly acquires stolen goods as a gift or in a commercial exchange may be required to give them up because of what the law calls 'unjust enrichment'.

The third principle may require a victim to be compensated even when the perpetrator is not in the position to pay. States sometimes undertake the responsibility of compensating victims of crime.

In Aristotle's account, the requirements of reparative justice are fulfilled when a judge forces the perpetrator to return what he has stolen. But even in legal contexts this does not suffice. Wrongdoers are expected to acknowledge responsibility for their deeds, to show remorse, to apologise or demonstrate in some other way that they owe a moral debt to their victims. Perhaps because reparative justice has usually been regarded as a legal matter, traditional accounts treat this additional requirement on wrongdoers as something separate from reparation itself. But from a moral point of view, acknowledging responsibility is intrinsic to reparative justice. An injustice, says Margaret Urban Walker (2010), is an act of disrespect that undermines trust and destroys confidence in the existence of shared standards. Genuine remorse, admission of guilt, an apology, or other acts that demonstrate to victims that wrongdoers acknowledge and are sorry for what they did are means of repairing the damage that injustice does to social relationships.

When wrongdoers are willing to take responsibility for their wrongs, victims may be prepared to forgive. By acknowledging their wrongs perpetrators can contribute to a process of reconciliation. Reparation is not the same as reconciliation. Perpetrators can owe reparation even if there is no prospect of reconciliation with their victims. They are obliged to acknowledge their wrong but victims are not required to accept their apology or forgive them. Reconciliation might be achieved by means other than reparation. But making acknowledgement of wrong into a requirement of reparation brings the aims of reparation and reconciliation closer together.

Acceptance of responsibility plays an especially important role when there is no compensation that can repair the wrong done. There is no way of undoing a murder and no payment that will repair the harm done to families and other survivors. Often the most meaningful thing that a perpetrator can do in the eyes of survivors is to show contrition.

Whatever form it takes, reparative justice consists in the obligations and entitlements that result from the commission of an injustice. The obligations are owed by those who are responsible for remedying the wrong of the injustice and the entitlements belong to those who count as its victims or survivors. Reparative justice is different from retributive justice: from principles about appropriate punishments for crime. Some perpetrators of injustice are rightly punished for their deeds but this debt to society is different from their obligation of reparation to their victims. Reparative justice is also different from distributive justice: principles governing the distribution of resources and opportunities in a society and in the world as a whole. Distributive justice is about the benefits that people owe to each other because they are members of a society, or simply because they are members of the human race. Reparative justice is about what is owed for wrongdoing.

Historical Injustices and Reparation

Slavery of the eighteenth and nineteenth centuries is an historical injustice. It was a wrong committed by people of the past against people who are also now dead. The death of perpetrators does not necessarily eliminate reparative responsibilities. The debt for a wrong done by someone now deceased may be charged to his estate – thus passing on the responsibility for reparation to his heirs. Debts may also be charged to corporations and other groups that continue to exist through changes of membership. German companies are contributing to a fund to pay reparation to those they used as slaves during the Nazi period even though their present executives and employees had nothing to do with this crime. The death of victims does not necessarily eliminate reparative entitlements. Heirs of Holocaust victims are generally regarded as the rightful recipients of property stolen from their parents. Nevertheless, reparative claims for a wrong so ancient as slavery invite objections. How can these claims remain legitimate over such a long period of time? How can any person or group now have a responsibility for making reparation and how can anyone be entitled to receive it?

Advocates of reparation for slavery need to answer these questions as well as meeting other objections. In the following chapter I will examine arguments for and against reparation for slavery and the slave trade. But a discussion of reparation for a historical injustice stands in need of its own justification. Why should we concern ourselves with injustices that happened long ago? Why not concentrate on overcoming present injustices and making society better for existing and future citizens (Vernon 2003; Wenar 2006)? Those who think that demands for reparation for historical injustices are misconceived often add that concentration on relieving present injustices is better for descendants of victims. It encourages them to look to the future rather than to waste their energy feeling resentful and victimised.

This objection has its merits. Those who look backward on the injustices of the past sometimes miss opportunities to improve their lives in the present. But telling people that they should ignore the injustices that were inflicted on members of their families or communities is neither helpful nor morally sensitive. Historical memory plays an important role in the lives of members of families, nations, ethnic and racial groups. Individuals derive an understanding of their status and place in the world from the history of their group. If the history of their people is one of subjection and oppression, this is likely to have an adverse effect on their view of themselves and their relationships. Citizens who take pride in their nation's history should not be surprised when those who have suffered from a history of oppression ask them to face up to the injustices it has done.

Even those who are not interested in history cannot escape its effects. Historical injustices can cast a long shadow. They can be responsible for psychological as well as material harm passed on through the generations. Randall Robinson (2000), an American advocate of reparation, argues that the legacy of slavery has had a debilitating effect on African Americans. Slavery, he says, destroyed the heritage of the Africans who were transported to the New World. It took away their connection to a tradition that gave people a secure identity. Because former slaves and their descendants were not able to find a secure and respected place in American society this loss was never repaired. He thinks that the attitudes and behaviour of African Americans have been negatively affected by a history of loss, rejection and denial of true belonging.

Not all historical injustices have lasting effects. The wounds of history can be healed. This is most likely to happen when descendants of victims are able to prosper in a society that treats them fairly and extends to them the same opportunities that others enjoy. In these circumstances, their history becomes a narrative with a happy conclusion. But this has not happened in the case of slavery either in the United States or in African and Caribbean countries that are still struggling with the legacy of slavery and colonialism.

However, the fact that the bad effects of historical injustice can be overcome in the course of time through just dealings and improved standards of living for victims and their descendants encourages the belief that what is needed is not reparation but improved relationships, an appreciation of the historical causes of present disadvantages and an application of the principles of distributive justice.

One problem with this view is that the psychological effects of slavery that Robinson emphasises would not necessarily be removed by an improvement in standard of living. And many of those who demand reparation do not merely want material compensation. They also demand an acknowledgement of responsibility from the nation or group that did the wrong – not only for their own sake but also for the sake of their ancestors who died without recompense for the wrongs that they suffered.

A fairer distribution of resources would not eliminate an entitlement to reparation in the form of apology or some other symbolic acknowledgement of responsibility for injustice. It would also not necessarily eliminate an entitlement to monetary reparation or return of property. If someone has been unjustly dispossessed then he ought to obtain restitution. If someone commits a wrong then she ought to surrender her illicit benefits. Wealth gained as the result of good fortune or government benefits does not annul this requirement. Suppose that Haitians had recently discovered vast mineral wealth on their island and used it to make themselves rich. This change in their situation would not wipe out whatever reparative obligations are owed to them by France. If France ought to return the indemnity it forced Haiti to pay back in the early nineteenth century, then Haiti's newfound wealth would not erase this debt. Out of generosity or for the sake of good relations, Haitians might be prepared to forego payment. But that would be up to them.

To make entitlement to reparation subordinate to the requirements of distributive justice is to make it hostage to differing views about what is distributively just. Some people believe that wealth in our society ought to be redistributed so that there is a smaller gap between rich and poor. Others do not think that this gap is unfair. They think that people deserve the wealth they have acquired by their efforts. Or they believe that people have a right to what they legitimately own and are entitled to transfer their wealth as they please – a position advocated by those who call themselves libertarians. Those who have these desert-based or libertarian ideas about justice do not support a redistribution of resources in their society apart from (at most) providing a safety net for the very poor.

The view that justice does not require much in the way of redistribution of resources prevails in international affairs. Cosmopolitans argue that the wealth of the world should be more equitably distributed, but most people believe that wealthy nations are entitled to retain their resources and use them as they please, having at most an obligation to aid countries that are very poor or are suffering from a disaster.

If reparative justice for historical wrongs must give way to the requirements of distributive justice, then those who are suffering from the effects of their history cannot expect much to be done for them in societies where inequality is tolerated. This is a practical reason for refusing to abandon reparative claims. But people also have moral reasons for taking demands for reparation seriously, whatever their views about distributive justice. Reparation is about responsibilities and entitlements that do not necessarily depend on how wealth is now distributed. But even when those who argue for reparation require no more than what would be brought about by an application of principles of distributive justice, their demands are not irrelevant. Obligations of reparation have weight. Arguments for reparation add force to demands for reform and they also require that special attention be paid to those who count as victims of injustice.

People who believe that distribution of wealth should be based on desert or who defend rights of property and inheritance have an especially good reason for taking reparative claims seriously (Butt 2008). Those who think that people should be rewarded according to desert should not assume that their wealth is deserved if some of it is the result of earlier injustices. Those who believe that their entitlement to what they now possess comes from their right to inherit cannot dismiss the claim that descendants of slaves are the rightful inheritors of resources that were wrongly denied to their ancestors. And citizens of nations who believe that the industry or legacy of their predecessors gives them an entitlement to their national wealth cannot justifiably ignore claims that some of it rightly belongs to nations that were wronged by these predecessors.

Demands for reparation for slavery should be taken seriously. But that doesn't mean that they are justified. All claims for reparation for historical injustices raise difficult issues about responsibility and entitlement. Demands for reparation must surmount the objections of those who doubt that anyone now possesses an obligation to make reparation or has an entitlement to receive it. They must explain why demands for reparation for slavery remain relevant when so much has happened since slavery ended. They must explain why descendants of slaves and former slave colonies, or their leaders, should not be held responsible for their present disadvantages and why Africans deserve reparation when some of their ancestors dealt in slaves.

Those who demand reparation for slavery must also provide a justification for their particular claims. The case they can make depends crucially on the nature of their demands, on historical events and on present circumstances. A discussion of reasons for accepting or rejecting demands for reparation for slavery must keep particular examples in mind. In the following I will focus on the three that I have introduced in this chapter: the demand of Haiti for reparation from France for the indemnity it was forced to pay; the demands of West African countries for reparation from Great Britain and other European nations for the slave trade and colonialism; and the demand for reparation for slavery by descendants of slaves in the United States.

2

Should Current Generations Make Reparation for Slavery?

Present citizens of the United States, Britain and France did not put Africans on slave ships or force them to work on plantations. Descendants of slaves living in America and Haiti were never enslaved and present citizens of West African countries have not had their lives and families disrupted by slave traders. Those who demand reparation for slavery need to explain why people have reparative obligations for injustices they didn't commit and why others have reparative entitlements for injustices they didn't suffer.

The claim that descendants of slaves are entitled to reparation also faces a problem about identity. Which individuals come into the world depends on who their parents are and this depends on the factors that bring people together and result in the conception of children. The children born to slaves in the New World were not likely to be the same as the children who would have been born if their parents had remained in their villages in Africa and married someone in their community. What individuals were born in the next generations was also affected by the social and personal circumstances of slaves or former slaves in America and former slave colonies. This means that present descendants of slaves would almost certainly not be in existence if slavery and the slave trade had not occurred. How then can they claim reparation for a wrong to which they owe their existence? How can they claim to be worse off because of that wrong?

Explaining how present people can be responsible for reparation for slavery or how they can have a right to reparation requires understanding what it means to be responsible for an injustice or to have reparative entitlements. David Miller (2007: 83–4) identifies two kinds of responsibility for past events. The first, outcome responsibility, belongs only to those who played a causal role in bringing something about. We generally assign the duty of reparation to those who have outcome responsibility for an event that causes unjust harm. But reparative obligations can also be assigned to individuals because of their role, situation or their relationship to agents with outcome responsibility.

They have what Miller calls remedial responsibility. People can have remedial responsibility for reparation because their role in an organisation requires them to take responsibility for what it did in the past. Individuals or groups can also be assigned remedial responsibility because they benefited from a wrong or because they possess something that rightly belongs to the victims. Present people have no outcome responsibility for slavery in the eighteenth and nineteenth centuries but they might have responsibilities of a remedial kind.

An entitlement, like a responsibility, can be acquired in more than one way. People have an entitlement to reparation when the actions or negligence of others cause them harm or loss. But they may also acquire an entitlement because of their status. They can have a status entitlement because they are members of a family, community or nation that is entitled to reparation or because they are heirs of victims of injustice. Their right to reparation in such cases depends on membership or their relation to others and not how they came into being. The fact that they might not have existed if the injustice had not been done does not affect their entitlement as an heir or as the member of a wronged group.

Individuals may also have a status entitlement because they belong to a class of people who are wronged by the failure of others to fulfil moral or legal requirements (Winter 2006; Meyer 2006). Suppose builders of an apartment block ignore safety standards and fifty years later it collapses, injuring many residents. Those entitled to reparation include individuals born after the building was constructed, even those who wouldn't have been born if their parents hadn't lived in it. They too belong to a class of people who are entitled to the protection of building codes.

Present people in America, Haiti and Africa are not victims of eighteenth- and nineteenth-century slavery. Nevertheless, they may be able to claim an entitlement to reparation because of their status as heirs of their forebears or as members of a family, community or nation. Or they may be able to claim reparation because, like the inhabitants of the apartment block, they belong to a group of people who are suffering the effects of past failures of governments or corporations to meet moral or legal standards. If they can claim reparation because of their status, then the likelihood that they would not have been born if slavery had not existed is irrelevant.

However, accusing past people of moral failure invites another criticism of reparative claims. Let's assume that those who owned slaves or engaged in the slave trade did not think that they were doing anything morally wrong. They were simply acting according to the law and morality of their day. People who have no means of knowing that their actions are wrong should not be blamed for moral failure. How then can reparation be owed for what they did?

Defenders of reparation can point out that it is implausible to suppose that slave traders and slave owners had no means of knowing that their actions were morally questionable. Reasons for condemning slavery were widely available in Western societies throughout the time when slavery existed, and opponents of slavery did not keep their views to themselves. But the more important point is that the guilt or innocence of our forebears does not affect our reparative responsibilities. Slavery is wrong. Our reasons for this belief apply to slavery in earlier centuries as much as they do to slavery as it now exists. Blameable or not, slave owners and traders committed an injustice for which reparation may now be owed.

The fact that the perpetrators and victims of eighteenth- and nineteenth-century slavery are long dead does not rule out reparative claims. Nor does the purported innocence of slave owners and traders. But it does not follow that these claims are justified. In the following sections I will present the three main arguments for reparation for slavery and the slave trade. The first appeals to right of inheritance, the second to the benefits obtained from slavery, and the third to the continuing harm that it causes. My objective is to determine whether these arguments can meet the challenges of those who oppose reparation for slavery and to determine how they apply to the three cases for reparation that are a focus for my investigation.

Argument from Inheritance

Slave owners forced people to work without pay. An individual's ability to labour is a possession that by right belongs to him or her. They are entitled to use it for their own purposes or to sell it to an employer. Slavery is a form of theft.

Haiti as a newly independent country was forced to pay an indemnity to former plantation owners in France. These slaveholders gained their wealth from wrongfully expropriating the labour of slaves. Some (if not all) of the money paid to France rightfully belonged to former slaves and their families.

The first principle of reparative justice requires restitution – the return of a resource or property that was wrongly taken from its rightful possessor. How much slaves should have been paid can be estimated from records of the hours they worked and the average wage that was paid at that time to free workers (Craemer 2015). According to the argument from inheritance, this money, plus the interest it would have earned if it had been invested at a standard rate, is now owed to the descendants of slaves – the rightful inheritors of what should have been paid to their ancestors.

Inheritance is usually thought of as a family matter – the passing down of wealth from forebears to their descendants. But the argument for inheritance can also be applied to intergenerational groups like nations. If Haiti was wrongly required to pay an indemnity to France then the right to restitution has been passed down by each generation of Haitians to their successors. Present members have the entitlement because they are the political heirs of those who were wronged.

There is another way of stating the argument from inheritance. After the American Civil War, the United States government should have made reparation to former slaves. Thaddeus Stevens' bill would have given former slaves land that had belonged to slave owners, but Congress did not pass it. Descendants of slaves are thus owed a monetary equivalent of the reparation that their ancestors failed to receive, adjusted to reflect its present value.

Bernard Boxill argues that the right to reparation of descendants of slaves gives them a claim not only to property of former slave owners but also to a share of the property inherited from all those who 'assisted, concurred or consented to their transgressions' (2003: 74). Since most white Americans consented to slavery and since they passed on their property to other white Americans, including immigrants who arrived after the Civil War, he thinks that descendants of slaves have inheritance rights over a share of what white citizens now possess.

The case for claiming reparation as a right of inheritance depends on what this right is. For Robert Nozick, right of inheritance is implied by the existence of a right to possession that ought not to be curtailed or abridged by the actions of others or the policies of governments (1974: 150–3). A person's right of ownership allows her to sell her possessions or bequeath them as she wishes. If they are unjustly taken from her then she and her heirs have a right to restitution that is not limited or annulled by the passage of time or changes in political or social conditions. Nor does it depend on the continued existence of the dispossessors or whether they have retained what they owe. If the resource in question has been absorbed into the economy of a society (as has the wealth of former slave owners and traders) then members of the society owe the debt – not because they have done anything wrong or benefited from injustice but simply because the heirs of the victims have a right to restitution.

Nozick's account of right to possession and inheritance provides the best basis for claims to reparation as the rightful inheritance of descendants of slaves. We have no way of knowing what slaves would have done with their wages or their land if they had received reparation. We can't know if they would have chosen to pass on their possessions to their children. We don't know what would have happened to this wealth in later generations. But this lack of knowledge should not be used to deny restitution to descendants. By law and custom we assume that descendants are the rightful heirs of their forebears unless there is reason to suppose otherwise.

A right of possession that persists through time and change faces an obvious difficulty. The land that grew cotton in the American South was seized by American colonists from indigenous people. The natives of Haiti, after whom the country is named, were dispossessed and killed by Spanish invaders and the Spanish were ousted by the French. If the plantation lands of the American South and the Caribbean were not the rightful possessions of slave owners, if they unjustly enriched themselves by the use of stolen property, then their entitlement to use their gains to pay wages comes into doubt and so does the entitlement of descendants of slaves to receive an inheritance. Perhaps we could insist on a temporal cut off point for reparation claims, though any choice of dates would be arbitrary. The question remains whether we should accept a view of right to restitution that is so blind to social changes and the interests of present people.

The justification for right of possession, according to Jeremy Waldron (1992: 18–19), is to ensure the security of individuals and to provide them with a stable basis for planning their lives. When people are wrongly dispossessed their lives are disrupted and restitution is clearly required. But this right, says Waldron, is subject to supersession. If decades have passed and those who wrongly appropriated a resource have become dependent on it, if it has become central to their plans and expectations, then it would be unfair to force them to give it up. It would be especially unfair to force people who are merely descendants of the perpetrators to give up a possession that has been incorporated into their lives. And those who earlier had a legitimate reparation claim can no longer insist that possessing it is central to their lives. They have had to make other arrangements.

Waldron does not discuss reparation for slavery but it is not difficult to use his view about supersession to challenge inheritance claims of descendants of slaves. Former slaves should have been paid for the value of their labour. The United States government after the Civil War should have ensured that reparation was extracted from former slave owners by giving some of their land to former slaves. Former slaves had a right to plan their future on the basis of receiving this money or land. But it was wrongly denied to them, and they and their descendants had to find another basis for their future. Meanwhile the descendants of slave owners and other innocent people who now hold the resources that should have been given to slaves are entitled to assume that they can depend on secure ownership to plan their lives. The injustice of failing to pay slaves for the value of their labour or to give them land has been superseded by changed conditions and the needs of present people. The right to restitution has faded away.

The same reasoning might be used to deny restitution to West Africans and Haitians. The British and other Europeans extracted people and wealth from

African communities, first through the slave trade and then through colonialism. The French extracted resources from Haiti that rightfully belonged to its people. But the resources gained from these injustices now belong to innocent people who use them for their own legitimate activities. Meanwhile Africans and Haitians have found other ways of going on with their lives. Their right to restitution has also faded away.

Should we accept these conclusions? Waldron is surely right to insist that entitlement to restitution can fade away. No one can reasonably suppose that descendants of the Saxons (even if they can be identified) are owed restitution for property expropriated from their ancestors as the result of the Norman conquest of England in 1066. But it doesn't follow that all restitution claims made by descendants of victims should be dismissed. Some injustices are resistant to supersession and some restitution claims of descendants may be justified even when the injustice was done many generations ago.

Members of indigenous communities in Canada, the United States, New Zealand and Australia have been able to claim some of the land that was stolen from their ancestors in the eighteenth and nineteenth centuries. One reason for the success of their claims is that they made a demand on behalf of their group against the nation that dispossessed their ancestors. Both victims and perpetrators are communities that persist through the generations. A wrongdoer has a continuing responsibility to make restitution to the victim unless there is a good reason for not doing so. Passage of time is not in itself a good reason. Changing conditions can be good reason but only if restitution would now unjustly deprive people of something central to their life plans. This consideration explains why indigenous people are not entitled to get back everything that was possessed by their ancestors – all the land in North America, New Zealand and Australia. But it doesn't follow that they are entitled to no restitution at all. In response to indigenous claims, nations have generally been able to provide partial restitution in the form of government land and right to resources without significantly disadvantaging non-indigenous citizens.

Another reason why the right of indigenous people to restitution has not been superseded is because they can often demonstrate a persisting cultural attachment to the land of their ancestors. They can reasonably claim that dispossession has deprived them of something essential to their way of life and that their collective existence cannot be satisfactorily maintained without it. Even Waldron allows that indigenous land claims may persist for cultural reasons (1992: 19–20). But this consideration points to a more wide-ranging reason why demands for restitution can resist supersession. If victims of dispossession and their descendants are not able to find a satisfactory basis for their lives – if the deprivation caused by the injustice cannot be overcome – then it has not been superseded. The interests of present possessors should not override the interests of those who continue to suffer from the injustice. This is so even if these present possessors have themselves done nothing to oppress those who are disadvantaged.

Imagine a society where wealth is mostly transferred through inheritance and where ideas of distributive justice and equal opportunity do not apply. Rich families remain rich through the generations and poor families stay poor. Suppose also that the rich gained their wealth in the first place through an injustice done to the ancestors of those now poor. In this society injustice has not been superseded and claims for restitution by poor families have a moral justification. On the other hand, in a society where wealth is redistributed by means of taxes and welfare programmes and where the opportunities available to individuals are not much affected by their family origin, it is more difficult to justify demands for restitution by descendants of victims of injustice. In the generations since the injustice was done they have had opportunities to find a secure basis for planning their lives.

To sum up: demands for restitution for a historical injustice are most likely to be legitimate when perpetrators and victims are groups that have persisted through the generations, and when at least partial restitution can be made without significant detriment to the well-being and life plans of those who have to make sacrifices for the sake of justice. They also resist supersession when the social world of victims and their descendants has not provided them with means for recovering from the injustice. Given these guidelines, let us determine whether the argument for inheritance can be used to justify reparation to American descendants of slaves, to Haiti or to African communities affected by the slave trade and colonialism.

The case for restitution to American descendants of slaves depends either on families being groups that have persisting reparative entitlements (like indigenous tribes) or on reasons to believe that descendants of slaves have not had the opportunity to recover from the failure of their ancestors to receive what was owed to them.

A case for restitution that depends on inheritance rights of families rests on dubious grounds. It is true that restitution can be owed to descendants of victims. Children are often regarded as the rightful possessors of what was stolen from their now deceased parents. But law and custom in modern societies do not look with favour on the restitutive claims of great-great-great grandchildren of victims of expropriation. The reason is, perhaps, that family membership and family possessions do not in modern societies have such a long-term effect on the political and social status of individuals. The loss of a family possession is not likely to have fateful consequences for the standing, honour or rights of distant descendants. This is what makes Waldron's supersession thesis difficult to resist. Why should we disturb the status quo, upsetting the lives of innocent people, in order to ensure that present members of families can obtain what belonged to their distant ancestors?

However, an entitlement to restitution is likely to persist if the descendants of the victims lack an opportunity to recover from the loss suffered by their ancestors. For this reason, the poor in the imagined society have good grounds for restitution, and Boxill suggests that American descendants of slaves can make the same case. Those who owed restitution to former slaves kept their assets and passed them down to their children: 'The whole of each generation of whites passed on its assets to the whole of the next white generation because each generation of whites specified that only whites of the succeeding generation were permitted to own or compete for the assets it was leaving behind' (2003, 76). White monopoly over the assets of slavery, he suggests, has been detrimental to the descendants of those who were wronged by slavery.

Boxill can be accused of exaggeration. By sharing in the wealth and opportunities of their society black Americans share assets that derive from slavery. Some have been able to prosper. But even those who are poor receive transfers in the form of welfare from taxpayers. Whites have not been able to keep all the assets of slavery to themselves.

What makes Boxill's statement plausible is that blacks in American society are, on average, much worse off than whites. This disadvantage, I will argue, stems at least in part from the effects of continuing injustice. People or nations who commit injustices that disadvantage others or fail to act to overcome the effects of injustice cannot claim to be innocent possessors of wealth. But if their complicity in wrongdoing gives them a reparative obligation this is not because descendants of slaves have inherited a right to restitution from their ancestors. They have it because these descendants are themselves victims of injustice.

The best claim to an inherited right to restitution of our three cases belongs to Haiti. France extracted a large indemnity from Haiti, at least some of which was an unjust appropriation of resources that should have belonged to former slaves. France, the wrongdoer, is an agent with an obligation to pay its debts. It could excuse itself from its reparative responsibility if making restitution would seriously affect the legitimate interests of present citizens of France. But the burden of restitution on citizens of this wealthy country is not likely to pose a significant threat to their interests. Present Haitians are the political successors of those who were forced to pay the indemnity and their entitlement to receive reparation comes from their membership in the nation that was wronged for so many years. If we accept that wrongdoers have a continuing obligation to make restitution to their victims unless they have good moral reasons for not doing so, then these considerations are sufficient justification for Haiti's claim.

There is another consideration that adds weight to Haiti's demand for restitution. There are no requirements of distributive justice in international society. In the course of time France has offered some aid and concessions to Haitians but it is not obliged, according to customary ideas about justice, to share its wealth with Haitians and neither are other nations. Whatever disadvantages paying an indemnity caused to Haiti have not been removed by transfers of wealth from the perpetrator to the victim. It would be difficult to determine whether, or how much, payment of the indemnity is responsible for Haiti's present poverty. Haiti has had a history of civil strife, dictatorship and natural disaster. But it is reasonable to assume that having to pay such a large amount of money over such a long period of time had an adverse effect on its ability to develop its economy and enable its citizens to live better lives.

This case for reparation raises basic philosophical questions about agency and responsibility. Why should we suppose that nations of today are the agents that bear responsibility for injustices of past officials and governments? This is an especially critical question when a nation has undergone radical political changes, as did France during the eighteenth and nineteenth centuries. And why should present citizens bear a burden, however small, for injustices committed by officials and governments of the historical past? We need an explanation for assigning remedial responsibility to them. All the arguments for reparation examined in this chapter raise these questions, and they will have to be answered. But meanwhile let us be content with the observation that the reparative responsibility of nations and their citizens is taken for granted not only in international law but also in most discourses about political obligations and entitlements. French officials assumed for over a hundred years that their nation had a right to extract reparations from Haiti. Problems about identity and agency over time and change did not worry them. And they did not doubt that Haitians of succeeding generations should bear the burden of the debt. In making their case for restitution Haitians can rely on the same presumptions about identity and responsibility.

Can Africans make a similar case for restitution? Europeans who engaged in the slave trade took young men and women who were lost to their families and communities. The economic effect of this loss is hard to estimate. But the slave trade also caused many communities, especially those that traded in slaves, to become economically dependent on Europeans. The vulnerability of African societies, as well as the loss to Europeans of the profits of the slave trade, were factors that encouraged the Europeans to colonise Africa in the nineteenth century. The wrongs of slavery and colonisation are difficult to separate. If we treat them together, as do Africans who make demands for reparation, it seems possible for some African communities to claim restitution for the gold, chromium, palm oil, copper, platinum, diamonds and other resources expropriated from their territories by the British and other European colonists.

However, those who use the argument from inheritance to demand restitution to Africa face a number of difficulties. Some of the political communities from which slaves and resources were taken no longer exist and it is not obvious that present African nations have inherited their right to restitution. Nigeria, for example, contains communities that were victims of slave hunters, but it also contains people whose ancestors hunted and exported slaves. Moreover, some of the resources expropriated by the colonial powers were not then of much value to Africans. If restitution depends on what African leaders would have asked in payment for these resources at the time they were taken, the debt would probably not amount to much even if interest were added to the sum. Another argument for reparation will serve Africans better.

Argument from Unjust Enrichment

The people of the United States, in the North as well as the South, benefited from the wealth produced by slavery. British slave traders and people who made goods for the slave trade or manufactured products from raw materials produced by slaves were beneficiaries of slavery and so were those who supplied them or bought their wares. Wealth generated by slavery spread through European economies benefiting almost everyone and it was passed on in one way or another to succeeding generations. The second argument for reparation for slavery and the slave trade invokes the second principle of reparative justice: beneficiaries of slavery and the slave trade ought to surrender what they have unjustly gained.

The second principle does not tell us where the surrendered benefits should go. But the most appropriate recipients are those whose families, communities or nations have been adversely affected by the injustice. To justify reparation as divestment of unjust benefits, it is not necessary to establish that descendants of slaves or present West Africans have inherited an entitlement to reparation or that their present disadvantages are all the result of the original injustice. The political community that suffered the injustice need not be in existence. Benefits from an injustice might be justifiably transferred to descendants of slaves or Africans simply because they have been denied their fair share.

The argument from unjust enrichment gives individuals or groups a remedial responsibility for reparation because they have benefited from an injustice. Any way of benefiting from slavery – through trade, manufacture, employment or consumption – might be sufficient to make people and their descendants or successors into beneficiaries. Beneficiaries include not just those who directly benefited from slavery and their descendants, but also those who arrived later and took advantage of the wealth of their new society. Immigrants who came to America after the Civil War count as beneficiaries of slavery, as do their descendants.

Perpetrators of injustice ought to surrender their ill-gotten gains. This requirement is uncontroversial. It is much more contentious to claim that people innocent of an injustice should surrender their benefits, especially if they did not ask to receive them (Fullinwider 2002). The existence of an obligation to surrender benefits becomes even more controversial when assets gained from an injustice have passed through many hands and are now incorporated into the lives of individuals who assume they are entitled to use them for their own purposes. Waldron's view about supersession seems to apply to the second principle of reparative justice just as well as the first.

Nevertheless, the conviction that it is wrong to retain the fruits of an injustice has a strong appeal. Daniel Butt (2008: 127–8) thinks that it answers to our sense of justice. We should want justice to prevail and injustices to be repaired, he says. We contribute to just outcomes by surrendering the benefits of an injustice and using them to repair the harm it has done.

This appeal is more effective in some contexts than in others. People all over the world obtained benefits from slavery, including child workers in Manchester cotton factories and people who were employed in industries that traded with firms that profited more directly from the slave trade. Some of the beneficiaries lived in non-slave-owning or trading countries. The sense of justice of their descendants is not likely to direct them to give up whatever benefits might have come down to them.

The appeal to a sense of justice is more persuasive when the beneficiary is an agent who contributed to the wrong. If a company obtained some of its present resources through investing in slavery or making some other contribution to its existence, then a proper sense of justice ought to direct it to surrender some of its wealth – perhaps donating it to projects that aid African Americans, Caribbean people or Africans.[4] The appeal may also be effective when benefits gained by those who did wrong are handed down in a family from generation to generation. Current descendants of slaveholders or slave traders might be moved to make reparation to descendants of slaves – particularly of those owned or transported by their ancestors, if they can be identified. Those who are so motivated are likely to be people who care about the history of their family or identify with some of their ancestors. Those who do not have this identification are less likely to be moved. In any case, an appeal that depends on family connections does not reach those who benefited merely by the greater prosperity that slavery or the slave trade brought to the economy of their country.

The appeal to a sense of justice is most likely to succeed when a corporation or nation has acted over the generations to ensure that wealth obtained from an injustice is retained for the benefit of its members and when the descendants or successors of those to whom the injustice was done have been

[4] In 2002 a class action was mounted against some American corporations that had profited from slavery. The courts refused to hear the case, but it could be argued that these companies have a *moral* obligation to surrender their unjust benefits.

excluded from benefiting. In this plausible version of the unjust enrichment argument, merely benefiting from a historical injustice is not enough to generate an obligation. The obligation to surrender benefits belongs to members of a group who have used its institutions to keep the fruits of an injustice for themselves, thus denying them to descendants of those who were wronged. The argument does not require that beneficiaries retained their benefits by unjust means. The institutions that enabled them to keep their wealth for themselves may be universally regarded as just. But the argument from unjust enrichment is even stronger when the means used to retain the benefits are unjust. In these cases the original injustice is compounded by further, more current, injustices and the case for surrender of unjust gains becomes especially compelling.

Black Americans have not shared equally in the wealth derived from slavery. If they have been denied a fair share because it has been monopolised by whites (as Boxill argues), then presently existing white Americans have been unjustly enriched and blacks have been unjustly deprived. This would be so even if these whites are not now committing any injustices against blacks. But the argument from unjust enrichment cannot be confined to making a case for reparation to black Americans. The

American nation and American wealth was made possible by the dispossession of indigenous people. Injustices were done to other groups in the course of building the nation. Much of American wealth probably counts as unjust enrichment. In this context the argument from unjust enrichment becomes an argument for redistribution of national wealth: taking from those who have been most advantaged by past injustices and giving it to those who are the least advantaged. Most black Americans would benefit from this application of distributive justice but it would not really count as reparation for slavery.

However, in other contexts the argument from unjust enrichment provides a justification for reparation for slavery and not merely a reason for redistributing resources in favour of people who have been disadvantaged. The slave trade helped to make Britain wealthy. Many companies and individuals in this nation benefited and these gains were incorporated into the British economy, benefiting most citizens. Later the British benefited from colonising Africa and extracting some of its resources. It would be wrong to say that Africans received no benefits from slavery or colonialism. Some African chiefs and their families and communities acquired wealth from the slave trade. Colonialists built infrastructure and imported institutions that African nations continue to use. But the assets flowed mostly in one direction. Through the generations Britain and other European nations have retained, invested and capitalised on wealth generated from Africa. Africans have had little or no access to the benefits that derive from this history of exploitation. There are no global institutions of distributive justice that require wealthy nations to transfer some of their wealth to the people of developing nations. The aid that the British and other European countries have sometimes given to Africans is small compared to the wealth enjoyed by their citizens. The British and other Europeans through the generations have thus retained and used benefits they derived from slavery and colonialism while excluding as beneficiaries those to whom the injustices were done. This is reason enough for reparation on grounds of unjust enrichment. If, in addition, the British used unjust means to retain and augment the benefits they obtained from slavery and the colonisation of Africa through unfair trading agreements or political pressure then the case for reparation becomes even more compelling.

Britain and other European countries did not confine their exploitative activities to Africa. The argument from unjust enrichment could be used to demand a transfer of wealth from former slave trading and colonising countries to the peoples that they exploited – perhaps giving priority to those who are now the most disadvantaged. But African countries whose territories were the source of slaves and minerals have a good reason for regarding themselves as appropriate recipients of reparation. The resources extracted by the British rightly belonged to the African communities from which they were taken. This gives the nation states that now represent the people of these territories a claim to at least some of the benefits that derive from the exploitation of these resources (and not merely restitution equal to the value of the resources at the time they were taken). To make this claim it is not necessary that the political communities that once possessed the resources now exist. It is sufficient that existing African nations are suffering a loss because benefits derived from these resources are not now available to their people.

The argument from unjust enrichment provides a good case for reparation to African countries for the slave trade and colonialism. But it does not help those who think that descendants of slaves are owed reparation for slavery and not merely a fairer share of the benefits of American society. Another argument may serve them better.

Argument from Continuing Harm

The proposal for reparation that Stevens presented to the American Congress might be interpreted as restitution for the wages that former slaves should have received. But it is better understood as an attempt to fulfil the third principle of reparative justice: that the harm caused to victims of an injustice should be repaired. The suffering and cruelty that former slaves had experienced could not be undone. It was not possible for them to return to the communities from which they or their forebears had been taken. They had lost contact with their African relatives and had been alienated from their traditional culture. Most had been born in the United States. But the harm of being enslaved could be repaired – so far as this was possible – by giving former slaves resources that would enable them to prosper as free American citizens. Present-day black Americans cannot claim compensation for being enslaved but they might be able to claim compensation for the harm caused to them by slavery or by the failure of federal and state governments to provide compensation for slavery.

Black Americans have fewer resources than American whites. On average blacks are at least twice as likely as whites to be poor or to be unemployed. Households headed by a black person earn on average little more than half of what the average white household earns. White households are about thirteen times as wealthy as black households. Blacks are less likely to get a college education and even among college-educated people blacks earn less than whites.[5]

Those who defend reparation for slavery often do so because they believe slavery to be the root cause of the disadvantages suffered by African Americans. Present-day African Americans are also victims of slavery, according to this view, and this gives them an entitlement to compensation for the harm it has caused them. Justification for this claim does not depend on whether white Americans have benefited from slavery. It does not rely on descendants of slaves having a right to inherit entitlements that were owed to their forebears. Reparation as compensation can be owed to black Americans who are not descendants of slaves so long as there is reason to think that they have been harmed by the consequences of slavery.

But slavery ended in the United States a long time ago and the claim that black Americans continue to suffer from its effects is open to question. Even

[5] This information is from Pew Research Center (2016).

some supporters of reparation doubt that slavery has much to do with the present situation of African Americans. Some prefer to rest their case for reparation on the Jim Crow laws in southern states that deprived generations of black Americans of civil rights and equal opportunities (Bittker 1973). Others think that reparation is owed for the harm done to black families by housing policies that denied to blacks federal grants and other benefits available to whites (Coates 2014). Others think that black Americans are owed compensation for the effects of unjust discrimination and unfair treatment that continue up to the present day (Fullinwider 2000; McCarthy 2004).

To discount slavery as a source of harm because it was succeeded by other injustices fails to take into account all the forms that an injury can take. Harm can be social and psychological as well as economic (Pierik 2006). People often care about the injustices inflicted on their ancestors. Thinking about these injustices causes them pain, sadness and sometimes resentment. But psychological harm does not depend on knowing or caring about ancestors. Robinson (2000), as we have seen, traces the alienation that he discovers in many black Americans – their pessimism, resignation and lack of connection to mainstream values – to the consequences of slavery. A historical injustice can have long-lasting effects on attitudes and social relationships.

Even in those cases where present harm can be traced to recent injustices, slavery may have played a critical role in making them possible. There are obvious causal relationships between slavery and more recent injustices. The laws that suppressed blacks in southern states were a reaction to the economic loss caused to whites by the end of slavery, to the large black population that was the result of slavery, to the fear of whites that former slaves and their descendants might become an overwhelming political force, and to attitudes that were a legacy of slavery. The interests, fears and attitudes that sustained these laws and other forms of oppression were an inheritance that one white generation passed on to the next (Acharya, Blackwell and Sen 2016).

Not all of the difficulties that African Americans encountered after the Civil War can be traced so directly to slavery. Federal legislation that denied blacks the same benefits that were provided to whites owed a lot to the influence of southern politicians, but the discrimination that blacks encountered when they went north to take advantage of opportunities in new industries may have been due to racial prejudice – something that can also be found in countries that have no history of slavery. Perhaps African Americans would have encountered prejudice and discrimination even if they had been free immigrants. But the presence of a large African American population in the United States was a legacy of slavery, not immigration. And racial prejudice itself, especially as it manifests itself in the United States, may have its origins in the attitudes and assumptions that made the enslavement of Africans possible. Justifying slavery, especially in a country founded on a belief in freedom, equality and natural rights, required a belief that Africans were inferior, dependent and animalistic in their impulses and desires. These assumptions are not easy to eradicate, especially when white people have an interest in maintaining their privileges.

There are good reasons for claiming that more recent injustices done to black Americans are linked directly or indirectly to slavery. To refer back to slavery when making their claims for reparation, it should not be necessary for black Americans to prove that slavery is responsible for all of their ills or that slavery is the sole cause of all of the injustices done to them. They can make their claim more precise and plausible by calling for reparation for a history of injustice that had slavery as a root cause.

This history of injustice encompassed not merely discrimination, exploitation and denial of rights but also the persistent failure to make reparation for slavery and other wrongs. Former slaves should have been provided with resources to enable them to overcome the harm of slavery. They should have been given the rights and opportunities of American citizenship and they should have been protected from those who wanted to deny them these rights. But this did not happen. No reparation was made to former slaves and governments failed to protect their rights. Some state governments took steps to perpetuate the subordination of former slaves and their families by restricting their right to own property, lease land, vote, or even to move freely in public spaces. The wrongful failure to compensate former slaves, compounded by these other injustices, was a harm to their children as well as themselves. These children were owed compensation for the harm caused to them by failure of their society to compensate their parents for slavery and for the wrongs that followed slavery. But they did not get what was owed to them and this injustice, along with other wrongs, harmed *their* children who were then owed compensation for the failure to make reparation to their parents (as well as for other injustices done to them). The continued failure to compensate black Americans has perpetuated harm through the generations. Present-day black Americans have an entitlement to reparation not merely because they are victims of a history of injustice rooted in slavery but also because they have been harmed by the continued refusal of their society to make reparation for slavery and for the injustices that followed slavery.

The American Civil Rights Law of 1964 outlawed discrimination on the basis of race. It ended segregation of schools and public facilities and prohibited restrictions on black registration to vote. This law did not end all forms of discrimination against African Americans, but it did provide them with more opportunities, augmented by affirmative action in favour of minority groups practised by some public institutions. Despite these reforms African Americans remain disadvantaged. Some of this continuing harm may be due to ingrained prejudices and institutional practices that have not been eliminated by civil rights legislation. But supporters of reparation have to counter the claim made by many of their opponents that black Americans have mostly themselves to blame for their present circumstances.

Basic to morality is the belief that individuals should be held responsible for their own actions or failures to act unless there is a good reason for excusing them. George Sher (1981) explains how having this responsibility can diminish the right to reparation. Suppose, he says, that a brilliant young man applies for admission to a law school but is rejected because of his race. The next year the law school ends its discriminatory practice, but the man, discouraged by his rejection, does not apply and instead takes a poorly paid clerical job. If he had entered law school he would have got his degree and a good job. Sher grants that being wrongfully rejected entitles him to compensation for loss of opportunity but insists that he is not entitled to the salary he would have earned if he had gone through law school. After all, he did not re-apply and he did not do the work that would have earned him a lawyer's salary. The man's son grows up in circumstances that are worse than those he would have had if his father had been accepted into law school. He may be entitled to some compensation, but far less than his father and it is not likely that members of later generations would be entitled to compensation at all. The injustice to their forebear has been superseded by the opportunities available to their parents and themselves and the choices they made or could have made. Opponents of compensation to black Americans might similarly argue that the advent of civil rights gave black Americans opportunities to improve their position and their failure to take sufficient advantage diminishes or entirely removes their right to compensation.

This objection raises questions about how much difference civil rights legislation and affirmative action have made to the lives and opportunities of most black Americans. But let us assume that the opponents of compensation are right to suppose that black Americans have not always taken advantage of available opportunities to improve their position. Choices, actions and failures to act can make a difference to reparative entitlements, but Sher's account of how injustices are superseded by new opportunities and the freedom of individuals to choose makes questionable assumptions.

Sher seems to assume that the injustice he describes is an isolated wrong, soon corrected, leaving no impediments to the young man's career. This makes his failure to re-apply to the law school into a personal failing. Sher's account ignores that fact that some injustices are systemic – affecting almost everything that victims do, the way that they think about themselves and their relations to others. It also ignores ways in which the effects of serious injustice can persist even when the wrong has ceased. American blacks experienced not merely the occasional denial of opportunity, but discriminatory practices that affected all aspects of their lives and their relationships with each other and with white Americans. They were taught to be inferior and to feel inferior. Nor did all the practices and attitudes that were part of the legacy of slavery and its aftermath go away as a result of the civil rights movement. Unjust institutions do not immediately become just, and even when those responsible for them are sincere about ending discrimination, past practices can have lingering psychological and social effects. They leave in their wake entrenched attitudes and assumptions, and habits of subordination and expectations of failure among former victims. Loss of trust, confidence and hope – the harms that Margaret Urban Walker (2010) identifies as a lasting legacy of systemic injustice – were evident in the attitudes and behaviour of the black Americans that Robinson encountered.

Moreover, the form discrimination took in American society has had adverse economic effects on black families that are not easily overcome. Laws and practices that prevented black families from owning property or denying them housing in areas with good services relegated many to neighbourhoods deprived of adequate infrastructure where their children were exposed to danger and not likely to get a good education. Such disadvantages tend to be passed down from one generation to another.

Another factor that Sher's emphasis on individual responsibility does not take into account is the role that governments played in the injustices done to former slaves and their descendants. What governments do, or fail to do, has a powerful and inescapable effect on the lives and opportunities of their citizens. If a government over a long period of time acts against the interests of citizens of a certain group, discriminates against them or fails to defend their rights, then there is little members of that group can do to avoid detrimental consequences for themselves and their families. Emigration for most people is not a viable option, and protest directed against groups supported by their government is difficult and dangerous, as supporters of the civil rights movement discovered. If people are treated over a long time as second-class citizens and objects of suspicion, then their distrust for the economic and social system that the government is supposed to defend is likely to become endemic – a legacy passed from one generation to another.

Entrenched disadvantages have a complex history. Some may be the result of bad luck, as in the case of the natural disasters that have devastated Haiti. Bad behaviour and bad management are likely to play a role. Even the most disadvantaged people are responsible for their own choices and some manage to overcome obstacles that are crippling to others. But it would be unfair to suppose that the responsibility of individuals for their actions undermines compensation claims for a history of injustice and denial of justice that has entrenched inequality and distrust in American society. Black Americans have a good case for reparation as compensation for the effects of a history of injustice and the persistent failure of their government and American institutions to make adequate reparation for harms that continue to affect their lives.

Responsibility for Reparation

I have argued that Haiti has a good case for restitution of the indemnity that it was forced to pay to France; that some African nations have a good case for demanding benefits that Europeans extracted from the slave trade; and that American blacks have a good case for demanding compensation for the continuing harm of a history of injustice rooted in slavery. All of these demands depend on the existence of an agent or agents who can be made responsible for reparation. Haiti, as we have seen, has claimed reparation from France, the nation that unjustly forced it to pay an indemnity. African countries similarly address their demands to the European countries they hold responsible for the slave trade and colonialism. Supporters of reparation for African Americans generally regard the United States government as responsible for making reparation, but they have also made demands of state governments that supported slavery, companies implicated in slavery, universities that made use of slave labour and churches that condoned and supported slavery.

Reparative demands are addressed to these groups because they are assumed to be agents with outcome responsibility for the injustices. Their policies, laws, decisions and actions either caused the wrong or contributed to it in a substantial way. Their institutions ensured that their members would benefit from the injustices and would retain these benefits through the generations. However, demanding reparation from these groups for the historical injustice of slavery raises three difficult issues.

The first issue is the one often raised by citizens of states. Why should they have to pay for the wrongs of past governments, officials and citizens? The second concerns identity. Agents have outcome responsibility only for what they do or for their negligence. If France is no longer the agent that imposed the indemnity on Haiti, if the Civil War changed the identity of the United States, if Britain has evolved into a different nation from what it was in the eighteenth century, then nations of today cannot have outcome responsibility for the injustices of eighteenth- and nineteenth-century slavery.

Even if we assume that the identities of France, the United States and Britain have remained the same through so much time and political change, the question remains whether it makes much sense to regard them as responsible for slavery and the slave trade. All three countries tolerated slavery for a long period of time and made laws that favoured and protected it. But the slave trade existed because it advantaged not only traders but also many other people in Europe and in colonies established by Europeans. These people, many of whom had considerable political influence, expected their government to support their enterprise and put pressure on it to do so. Slavery in the United States existed because it was profitable for southern plantation owners. It became ingrained in the culture of the American South and was accepted by most people as part of their way of life. In a democracy the will of a large number of citizens cannot be ignored. The United States government had to make compromises with those who supported slavery in order to keep the union together. When it ceased to satisfy those who wanted to expand slavery into new territories it faced rebellion and civil war. 'Slavery and its aftermath were social ills, not simply matters of public policy', says Iris Marion Young (2006: 177). Slavery and the slave trade are what she describes as structural injustices – wrongs that result from the interactions of many agents who are pursuing their own ends. When injustices are structural, she says, there is no point in looking for an agent to blame.

If presently existing nations cannot be held responsible for slavery it does not follow that demands for restitution or compensation are pointless. If France now has resources that really belong to Haiti then it should return them. If British citizens or companies have benefits that come from the slave trade and colonialism then a sense of justice should motivate them to surrender at least some of them to Africans. African Americans may be able to demand compensation from their government for harm resulting from a history of injustice even if the United States had little or no responsibility for the wrong of slavery. States sometimes take remedial responsibility for compensating victims of injustice. However, the force and plausibility of demands for reparation depend heavily on the belief that they are addressed to an agent with outcome responsibility – one that can be asked to acknowledge its wrongdoing and make amends. If there is no such agent then it becomes easier to believe that the injustice has been superseded or that alleviating its harmful effects calls for an application of distributive, rather than reparative, justice.

The first issue – the question about the remedial responsibilities of citizens for reparation for historical injustice – can best be answered by an account of why nations, corporations and other such groups should be regarded as agents that have responsibility for a past that extends beyond the lifetime of present members. This account must suppose that groups can act as agents. I go along with the common philosophical view that organised groups – groups that have institutions for making and carrying out decisions – can be agents if they are capable of consistency in their decisions and actions (List and Pettit 2011). To satisfy this requirement members have to abide by procedures for making decisions; they have to cooperate to carry them out and to take responsibility for their consequences, even when not all of them were in agreement about what was decided or voted for the officials who made the decisions. The agency of a group depends on members accepting collective responsibility for its procedures, institutions, policies and actions even when they do not agree with everything their group decides or does.

If a group is an intergenerational agent – if its identity as an agent persists beyond the lifetimes of those who are presently members – then its being responsible for its actions requires future members to take responsibility for the consequences of decisions that present members make through its institutions. It also requires present members to take responsibility for what was done by past generations. If, for example, their corporation or nation makes a long-term agreement with another corporation or nation then its members, present and future, have an obligation to fulfil it unless there is a good reason not to do so. If a nation wronged a family, community or another nation then its present members are responsible for reparation. When members wonder why they should bear the burden of reparation for their group's historical injustices they are asking why their nation or corporation has to fulfil the requirements of intergenerational agency.

Answers are both pragmatic and moral. Members of these groups rely on the consistency through time of their institutions and governing bodies. Their ability to make plans and enjoy security through the course of their lives depends on their group fulfilling undertakings it has made to them, maintaining institutions that continue to treat them fairly and remedying wrongs it has done. The persistence of a community in which the legitimate expectations of members of all generations can be fulfilled requires cooperation made possible by intergenerational agency. Each new generation must take responsibility for fulfilling, amending or repairing the effects of decisions of its predecessors and maintaining communal institutions.

People also have interests and desires about what will happen in the future beyond their lifetime. They care about the well-being of their children and grandchildren, the fate of their projects or the future of the ethnic, religious or tribal communities that they value. They rely on a group agent – a nation state – that is able to maintain its institutions and commitments through the generations and to take reparative responsibility for injustices that it sometimes does to families or communities. Many citizens also value their political traditions and institutions and think that they ought to be available for future generations. But those who believe that their group's traditions, constitution, practices and institutions ought to persist through the generations must, for the sake of consistency, accept the implications: that debts incurred as the result of the operation of these institutions must be paid, commitments of past governments must be honoured and reparation for injustice must be made unless there is a moral justification for not doing so.

The persistence of responsibilities through the generations, especially in political societies, is also a natural consequence of the fact that generations are overlapping. New members of nations generally enter as children, who are given the benefits of membership as a matter of course. They acquire the culture of the group and learn to accept the responsibilities of membership. They inherit the accomplishments of their predecessors but also the consequences of their unjust deeds.

After the Civil War the United States Congress unjustly failed to provide reparation to former slaves. Let us imagine that a referendum on reparation was put to white citizens in succeeding years and each time they refused to pay (Butt 2006). By doing so they acquire outcome responsibility for the injustice of refusing to make reparation. As the years go by, new citizens gradually replace those who had collective responsibility for slavery. But by voting no on the referendum they acquire responsibility for the injustice of refusing reparation. This situation does not change when there are no citizens left who were alive when slavery existed.

There were no referenda on reparation for slavery in the United States, but the failure of citizens to support reparation – to vote for Congressional representatives who would pass a reparations bill or to pressure them to do so – is sufficient to give present citizens collective outcome responsibility for the failure to make reparation for slavery.

But why should France, Britain or the United States be held responsible for something done when they had a very different political character? This question is especially pressing because these nations were not fully democratic in the eighteenth and nineteenth centuries. Britain and even the United States excluded some groups of people from voting. Nevertheless, the presumption of international law that nations normally retain their responsibilities despite changes of regime or an undemocratic politics answers to the interests of citizens as well to the requirements of international relations. The reasons for the existence of intergenerational agents capable of making decisions about the future and taking responsibility for the past are also reasons for the presumption that their responsibilities persist. What is important in most cases is not their form of government but the continuity of basic structures and practices, the ability of members to rely on the fulfilment of obligations and to maintain what they value for future generations. Even large political changes or the demise of a group agent do not necessarily bring their responsibilities to an end. A nation or corporation can be required to take over some of the commitments of its predecessor.

Does lack of democracy make a difference? Suppose a dictator borrows money and uses it to line his own pockets and to suppress his opponents until he is finally ousted by a popular revolution. Thomas Pogge (2002: 112–14) argues that it would be unfair to make the new democratic regime pay his debts. This conclusion is especially easy to accept because national debts are usually held by large financial institutions that should have known what the dictator would do with the money. But what if the dictator used the army and other institutions to dispossess a group of people so that his cronies could profit, or waged an unjust war on a neighbouring country that devastated their economy? Those who participated in these acts may have felt they had little choice. But they did the damage and if the new regime does not take responsibility for repairing the harm, who will? Persistence of responsibility is even harder to deny if the dictator's acts were favoured by many people in the population, if their participation was willing and if they profited from his deeds. It is especially hard to deny if leaders, democratically elected or not, have little choice but to act according to popular will.

Reparative responsibility does not disappear when injustices are structural. The interests, prejudices and customary practices of citizens are reflected in the laws and practices of a society and in the decisions that governments are constrained to make. And the laws and institutions of a society provide a framework that reinforces attitudes and customs, enables people to pursue their interests and limits or fails to put limits on what they can get away with in their treatment of others. If this treatment is unjust, then citizens are collectively responsible for the institutions that allow it. Through their active or tacit support, citizens of Britain and the United States were responsible for the persistence of institutions, laws, infrastructure, trading relations and commercial networks that made the slave trade and slavery possible for such a long period of time. Collective responsibility for slavery as a structural injustice belonged to them as citizens, and because of the requirements of membership in a nation that has to take responsibility for its deeds, the task of making reparation belonged also to those who did not support slavery, as it now belongs to present citizens.

However, Young is right to suppose that slavery was a cultural and not merely a political ill.

Many wrongs associated with slavery were part of everyday life in the American South. The attitudes that supported slavery and the oppressive system that took its place were widely accepted aspects of southern tradition. The cruelties of slave owners, the lynch mobs, the everyday oppression and other acts done by ordinary people to support an unjust system are beyond reparation. No one now can be required to take responsibility for them. But what people were able to do in support of slavery and white domination, what cruelties they were allowed to get away with, depended on what their federal and state governments as political agents gave them the power to do or failed to prevent them from doing. Reparation for these political acts or failures to act is the responsibility of citizens.

Objections to reparation for slavery have been answered. A good case can be made for restitution to Haiti, for transferring at least some of the benefits of the slave trade to Africans, and for compensation to African Americans for the continuing harms of slavery and related injustices. But the question of what they are owed remains, and the difficulties of providing an answer motivate further doubts about reparation.

3

What is Owed?

The principles of reparative justice tell us what reparation requires. Wrongly taken resources must be returned to their rightful owners. Those who have benefited from the injustice must surrender their gains, and the harm done to victims must be repaired. Victims and perpetrators must, so far as possible, be returned to the state they were in before the injustice was done.

In practice, the objectives of reparative justice are often impossible to fulfil. The expropriated resource or the benefit may no longer exist. The harm may be impossible to undo. The objectives of reparative justice are best thought of as an ideal that we ought to approach so far as possible. But this requires a method for determining what decisions about reparation come closest to the ideal. Historical injustices like slavery are difficult cases for reparative justice not only because of the issues raised by reparative demands but also because there seems to be no method for making an impartial, well-founded decision about what, if anything, victims or their descendants are owed.

To undo the harm done by an injustice or to identify the benefits it created we have to know what would now be the case if it had not been committed. This requires a historical reference point and a contrary-to-fact history. We have to first identify the point in time when the injustice occurred and then provide a plausible account of what would have happened to the victims and their descendants if it had not been done, or how those who benefited would have fared. In the case of slavery both these requirements seem impossible to fulfil.

Should we take as our reference point the early fifteenth century – the time before Europeans began enslaving people and trading slaves? Or would it be more appropriate to make it the early seventeenth century when the slave trade and slavery started to become a big business for Europeans? The contrary-to-fact histories would describe alternative worlds in which Europeans did not remove Africans from their communities, or at least did not remove very many. Either those who were enslaved by Europeans in the actual world would have remained in Africa and their descendants would presumably be living there, or they would have been enslaved instead by Arabs and their descendants would perhaps be living in a Muslim country. But these alternative worlds are so far removed from our actual world that they do not give us a guide to what reparative justice requires.

Perhaps the reference point should be the time when the slave trade was abolished by the British and Americans in the early nineteenth century or when they later abolished slavery. In the alternative worlds, slavery and the slave trade would have existed but African communities and former slaves would have received appropriate reparation for the injustices done to them. But there seems to be no decisive reason for choosing one reference point in preference to others, and people who can't agree on this matter are not likely to agree on what is owed in reparation.

Calculating the amount of unjust enrichment from slavery and the slave trade encounters the same problems. Does the unjust enrichment come from the benefits of importing Africans to work in tobacco, sugar cane and cotton fields in the New World or merely from their use as slaves rather than free labourers? Or should we concentrate on benefits resulting from the failure to make appropriate reparation to former slaves?

Even if people could agree on an appropriate reference point, the problems of constructing a plausible contrary-to-fact history remain. We have no way of knowing what would have happened to victims and their descendants, or to beneficiaries, if the injustices had not occurred or had been ended sooner, or if proper reparation had been made. If Africans had not been removed from their communities, if West African societies had not been traumatised or their economies distorted by the slave trade, then perhaps they would have embarked on their own road of economic development. Some African leaders and supporters of reparation claim that this is what would have happened (Babacar 2006). Or perhaps these societies and the standard of living of their members would have stayed much the same through the eighteenth and nineteenth centuries. If the slave trade and colonialism had never occurred or had been ended sooner then perhaps the British would now be much poorer. Or perhaps slavery and colonialism prevented the development of industries that would have provided more benefits to citizens. If Africans had come to America as free immigrants or had been freed much earlier, or if they had received adequate reparation, then perhaps their descendants would be on average as well off as the descendants of immigrants who arrived in the nineteenth century. Or perhaps Africans in America would have preferred to revive their cultural and communal life, as did many former slaves in Haiti. In that case, the outcome for their descendants might have been different from the outcome for descendants of immigrants from Germany, Sweden, Italy and other European societies.

The history of families and societies is affected by complex political and economic causes, the choices of individuals and group decisions. It is difficult to regard contrary-to-fact histories about the fate of Africans, white Americans or Europeans as anything more than poorly grounded speculation. How can reparative claims be based on such a flimsy foundation?

Reparation and Reconciliation

In practice, whether states or corporations pay reparation for a historical injustice and how much they pay is determined by political and legal considerations – by the relative power of the parties, the political pressure that victims or public opinion can exert, a desire to avoid conflict and by legal precedents. If victims feel that they have not been adequately compensated for the wrong, if descendants of victims object to being left out of consideration, there is not much they can do. They come up against legal requirements of proof of harm and all the other difficulties of determining to the satisfaction of legal or political authorities that something is owed to them.

I argued in the last chapter that descendants of victims of slavery and the slave trade can sometimes make a good moral case for reparation and that some perpetrators and beneficiaries of slavery have a moral obligation to acknowledge a reparative debt. But the reasoning that supports these conclusions is not likely to influence a court that puts the onus on claimants to establish beyond doubt that their present disadvantages are the result of the injustice. Their cases will not succeed if the law does not countenance entitlements of descendants or extend the category of 'unjust enrichment' to benefits received from distant predecessors. Since legal processes and precedents do not answer to the moral considerations that ground reparative obligations and entitlements for historical injustices like slavery, we need a different approach to reparative justice. We need a change of paradigm.

Aristotle, like most of those who discuss reparative justice, assumes that it is wholly backward-looking. Reparation requires correction to an imbalance in social affairs caused by injustice. It aims at a return to the state of affairs that existed before the injustice was done. For historical injustices like slavery a return to the formerly existing state of affairs is not only impossible – it would be morally undesirable. Waldron rightly points out that restoration of expropriated resources can unfairly disadvantage innocent people who have become dependent on ownership. Reparation that aims to return victims or descendants to a former state of affairs may also not be what they want or need. Descendants of slaves have interests that are different from those of their ancestors and most wouldn't want to be restored to the African community of their forebears even if that were possible. African communities are very different from what they were before Europeans exploited them and the people in them do not have the same interests as their ancestors. A plausible account of what is owed in reparation for slavery has to take into account the present interests and circumstances of both descendants of victims and descendants of perpetrators. The idea that reparative justice must be forward-looking is not unprecedented. When Stevens proposed that former slaves be given land and resources he aimed not merely to make up for their losses as slaves but also to ensure that they would have the opportunity to prosper as American citizens.

There is another reason for rethinking the purpose of reparation. A history of injustice is often responsible for psychological and social harms. It is a source of alienation and demoralisation, a cause of social division, fear, resentment and distrust. An adequate account of reparation for slavery and other historical injustices should emphasise mending relationships. It must take into account existing interests and conditions with the aim of removing the hindrances to good relationships caused by the injustices of history.

Moving from Aristotle's backward-looking account of the aim of reparative justice to a more reconciliatory approach is similar in some ways to a move from a retributive account of punishment that focuses on matching the seriousness of the punishment to the seriousness of the crime to one that emphasises forward-looking considerations like deterrence, reform of criminals and protection of society. A non-retributive conception of punishment takes into account the good or bad effects of punishment. A reconciliatory system of reparative justice takes into account present needs and relationships. A non-retributive system of punishment has the forward-looking aim of decreasing crime. A reconciliatory approach to reparation has the aim of overcoming the effects of an injustice by mending relationships.

Apology as Reparation

The reconciliatory strategy often adopted by states, corporations and other institutions in response to demands for reparation is official acknowledgement of wrongs done. Expressions of regret, apologies, memorial ceremonies, monuments to victims and other public demonstrations of contrition have become a common way of dealing with historical injustices.

Some critics regard these acts as mere symbolic gestures – a cheap alternative to reparative or retributive justice. But this view underestimates the importance of symbolism and it also ignores its reparative role. Walker (2010) argues that the act of truth telling that plays such a central role in truth and reconciliation processes is itself a form of reparation. By telling the truth and acknowledging to their victims that they did wrong, perpetrators address the harm caused to social relationships by injustice and contribute to the process of overcoming it.

Apology is a particularly effective method of performing this act of acknowledgement. By apologising perpetrators tell the truth to their victims: that they were the ones responsible for the harm or the loss. They admit the wrongness of their deeds and take responsibility. They express regret for what they did to their victims. By so doing they acknowledge the existence of the moral standards they violated and confirm that these standards apply to the relation between them and the victims. They give victims reason to trust and be hopeful about future adherence to them. An apology can be a powerful tool for repairing relationships.

Nevertheless, apology as reparation for historical injustice faces both moral and philosophical objections. Victims of injustice sometimes criticise apologies as a political means of avoiding *real* reparation – monetary compensation to victims or return of what was expropriated. Others doubt whether perpetrators of historical injustices can make meaningful apologies. The principal perpetrators of slavery and the slave trade – at least those that can now be held accountable – are intergenerational groups: corporations, churches and, above all, nations. But apologies made by officials or leaders of these groups are open to suspicion. How can an apology on behalf of a group be sincere if some of its members are not apologetic? Does it even make sense to suppose that a group can make an apology? Those who doubt the very possibility of group apology have in mind a standard that can be fulfilled only by an individual who remorsefully confronts her victim and asks her forgiveness.

A group cannot feel remorse. Apologies made on behalf of groups differ in this respect from apologies made by individuals. But a group apology is an act of agency that can fulfil the same function as apologies of individuals. Making an apology is something a group does as the result of a decision by its governing institutions, and the person who delivers it acts as a group agent. Her feelings and her relation to the injustice are irrelevant. Though a group apology is by its nature impersonal, it can give victims reason to believe that the group now respects moral standards and reason to trust and be hopeful about the future behaviour of its institutions and officials. There is no reason to doubt the legitimacy of an act of apology simply because it is made on behalf of a group.

However, trust and hope depend on the belief that group members will honour the decision. Victims of injustice have less reason for confidence if they continue to face prejudice and discrimination from unapologetic members of their community. The mere admission of wrongdoing by a person in authority can sometimes be meaningful to victims and their descendants. But to answer the moral objections often made about group apologies we need to know when an admission counts as genuine and when it is merely a political stunt or an inconsequential gesture.

Whether an apology of a group counts as genuine, whether it can heal damaged moral relationships, depends on what has been done to ensure that victims are able to believe and trust that its institutions will treat them with respect. They have little reason for this belief if a large number of group members do not admit that a wrong was done or if the apology is supported by only one political faction. Those who want their group to make a genuine apology must do the work of explaining to members why the apology is necessary and desirable. The most effective, believable apologies are those resulting from movements that build widespread popular support for a group apology. Apologies are more likely to be perceived as genuine by victims and their descendants if they are consulted about how they should be made. They are more likely to be meaningful if they have widespread political support and are delivered by the person who represents the group as a whole. This is why Americans who want an apology for slavery are not satisfied by Congressional apologies. They think that a proper apology must be delivered by the leader of the nation. Apologies are more likely to be regarded as genuine if they are followed by other acts: the building of memorials or monuments as reminders of the wrong done, commemorations, anniversaries and changes to official histories so that the injustice is not forgotten. They are more likely to play a role in healing damaged relationships if the group has already undertaken changes to unjust institutions.

An apology can remain a requirement of reparation even when material and social disadvantages caused by the injustice no longer exist. Let us imagine a different history for African Americans. Former slaves in this story received no reparation. But no further wrongs were done to them or their families. Though poverty at first held them back, their descendants were eventually able to take full advantage of the opportunities offered by their society and they encountered no barriers to the exercise of their rights as citizens. Black Americans prospered and there is now no reason to believe that they are disadvantaged in their civic life or economic activities by the legacy of slavery. Nevertheless, there is one reparative demand that they are entitled to make: that the wrong that was done to their ancestors should be officially acknowledged. If there is no acknowledgement of wrong done, if the injustice is covered up or treated as insignificant in official histories, then the descendants of victims of injustice remain uncertain about their place in society. They will lack the connection and identification with their nation and its history that is a valuable part of citizenship. In this respect they continue to suffer harm and an apology for slavery is an appropriate way of addressing it.

Beyond Apology

History did not go in the way imagined in this story. Further injustices were done to black Americans and I have argued that the disadvantages they now suffer can be traced to a history of injustice rooted in slavery. Apology is not enough. Apology is also not enough for the Haitians who have never been compensated for the indemnity that they were unjustly required to pay. And it is not enough for the African communities that never received reparation for the injustices that benefited others. An account of reparation for slavery and the slave trade has to explain what more is required in reparation and how this should be determined.

The reconciliatory approach eschews the aim of returning victims or perpetrators of a historical injustice to the situation they were in before the injustice took place. It responds to what descendants of victims now need and how members of perpetrating groups are now situated. An obvious proposal for dealing with reparative demands is to settle them by negotiation (Amighetti and Nuti 2015). An offer of reparation will count as fair if and only if the parties are fully represented, make an effort to appreciate each other's position, and are able to reach a democratic consensus about what is owed.

One obvious difficulty with this proposal is that discourse about reparation is likely to be less than ideal. In the real world, decisions often favour the stronger party. Needy victims have to settle for what they can get even if they think it unfair. Those who are able to get public opinion on their side are likely to do better than those whose claims are not so well publicised. But even when the parties are determined to make a fair decision, there is likely to be a disagreement about what this means. Participants need criteria for making judgements about fairness. Telling them that they should hold a discourse and make a democratic decision is not enough.

Moreover, this instruction misses the point of reparative justice. Those who demand reparation for injustices are not asking for assistance because they are needy. They make their demand because an injustice was done to them or their ancestors and they reasonably expect that reparation will answer to the seriousness of the wrong. A non-retributive theory of punishment cannot abandon the idea that severity of a punishment should be related to the seriousness of the crime. It would be wrong to hang a person for petty theft even if we thought that this would be a good deterrent. A reconciliatory approach to reparation can also not abandon the idea that the amount and kind of reparation should be appropriate to the wrong done. This means that we cannot reach a satisfactory conclusion about reparation for slavery without facing the problems of determining how much is owed.

A reconciliatory approach to reparation does not require exact answers to this question. It assumes that those who aim to repair relationships damaged by an injustice will also be prepared to negotiate and make compromises. But a reconciliatory approach does require guidelines, standards and reference points. It needs ways of distinguishing between reasonable and unreasonable demands or offers. Let us see if we can meet this challenge for the three cases that have been the focus of our attention: the demand of Haiti for a return of the indemnity paid to France; the demand of African communities for reparation from Britain and other European nations for the slave trade; and the claim of the descendants of American slaves for compensation for the harms of slavery.

Reparation to Haiti

Haiti was unjustly forced to pay an indemnity to France for appropriating the plantations of former slave owners. The injustice was compounded by forcing the country to borrow money from French banks at a high rate of interest. Eventually France decreased the amount Haiti was required to pay and in 1947 it forgave the remainder of the debt. The fact remains that it was wrongly imposed, and according to the first principle of justice France ought to restore what it wrongly took. There is no reason to think that this injustice has been superseded by the passage of time or changing conditions. International law normally requires that states pay their reparative debts even when they were incurred by past governments, and I argued that there are good moral grounds for regarding nations as agents with reparative responsibilities that persist through the generations and are not normally erased by political changes. If France had become a poor nation or if paying reparation would put heavy burdens on some French citizens, then there would be good reason to forgive the debt or decrease the amount the country has to pay. But France is not poor and given that its taxation system is reasonably fair, no French citizens would be made significantly worse off by contributing their share.

The claim that France ought to give back to Haiti what it wrongly expropriated does not depend on making a comparison between the present well-being of Haitians or the French and how they would have fared if the injustice had not happened. It does not depend on whether the Haitians would now be better off if they had not been forced to pay the debt. It does not depend on whether French citizens are now better off than they would have been if the indemnity had not been paid. It avoids the difficulties associated with contrary-to-fact claims. But it does not escape objections of other kinds.

What exactly does France owe? Former slaves were owed what should have been paid to them as wages. France ought to return to Haiti the share that should have gone to its people. But does it follow that France must return everything that Haiti paid?

The properties that the slave owners had to abandon were of considerable value and the wealth they produced was due partly to their own efforts and investments and not merely the labour of slaves. It is generally wrong for a state to expropriate private property without compensating owners. Did Haiti owe part of what it was forced to pay to France?

The second principle of reparative justice provides a clear answer to this question. People should not benefit from wrongdoing. The wealth of plantation owners in Haiti was gained through slavery. Moreover, these plantation owners supported and contributed to efforts to put down attempts by slaves to gain and keep their freedom. They had no moral justification for demanding compensation for lost property or income. It is true that the law at that time supported their claims, but this is not relevant to the issue of what France now owes Haiti. The law was unjust.

Expropriating wealth of wrongdoers becomes questionable when it leads to poverty and suffering, especially of innocent family members. But poverty was generally not a problem for former plantation owners. Many had wealth stashed away in French banks or investments. Others had support networks or alternative sources of income. But whatever hardship might have resulted to the families of slave owners, their agents and free employees, the agent responsible was not Haiti – a country that fought to liberate itself from the injustice of slavery – but the country that supported the slave economy in Haiti.

A moral debt caused by an injustice can be erased, or partly paid, by subsequent actions of the perpetrator. France, like many other wealthy nations, gives aid to Haiti, though it contributes far less than the United States or Canada. Does this exchange of wealth eliminate or reduce its reparative debt?

There is no reason to think that it does. If France provides aid to Haiti because nations have a moral or legal obligation to help those in need, satisfying this distributive requirement does not eliminate its reparative debt. People who satisfy requirements of distributive justice do not thereby eliminate or reduce reparative debts they have incurred to others. Let us suppose, however, that wealthy countries have no distributive obligations to poor countries. Whatever they give is charity – a matter of altruism. If France claims to be acting out of altruism in giving aid to Haiti (and receives due credit for its generosity), then it would be wrong for it to now declare that this aid pays its reparative debt. If France had at one time agreed to give special assistance to Haiti in return for relieving it of its debt and Haiti had freely consented to the arrangement, then the debt could have been paid by this means – providing Haiti was not forced to accept whatever offer France made. But this is not what happened.

There are thus no grounds for denying that France has a substantial reparative debt to Haiti. It ought to return all the money that Haiti was forced to pay. To compensate Haiti for losing the opportunity to invest this money in its own economy, France ought to pay interest on this sum equivalent to the rate it would have earned if it had been invested. France should also compensate Haiti for the unjust interest rates it was charged by French banks.

Is this all that France owes? Should it also compensate Haiti for the attempt during Napoleonic times to re-impose French rule and force Haitians back to slavery? Should other countries, the United States among them, compensate Haiti for denying it recognition and trade in the years after its revolution?

These claims are much more doubtful. The debt of restitution that France owes to Haiti does not depend on whether Haiti's present poverty results from being forced to pay an indemnity. France ought to return what it wrongly took. But making a case for compensation for the harm caused by Napoleon's forces or by other acts of foreign powers requires a reason for thinking that the people of Haiti continue to suffer from the consequences of these wrongs. This would be difficult to establish. There is, in fact, good reason for doubting that Haiti's present disadvantages are to any significant extent the result of what France or other powers did in the early nineteenth century. An independent nation has considerable means to determine the conditions in which its people live, their opportunities and level of well-being. If it has fertile land and other resources, it does not lack the means to recover from disadvantage. If a long time passes and it remains disadvantaged, there is reason to look for other causes: internal dissension, bad government, failure to provide an adequate education for its people or 'acts of God' like earthquakes and other disasters. Haiti has a good case for restitution of the indemnity it was forced to pay. But its case for compensation for harm caused by injustices committed over two hundred years ago is comparatively weak.

Reparation to Africa

The best case for reparation to Africans for the slave trade, as well as other injustices, focuses on the benefits extracted from Africa by Great Britain and other European powers from which Africans were largely excluded. It argues that at least some of these benefits ought to be surrendered and transferred to African communities harmed by this exploitation or to the nations that now represent these communities. But to determine what the British owe, if anything, we need a frame of reference and a contrary-to-fact history.

Suppose that Britain had not participated in the slave trade or colonised part of Africa. The reparation it now owes to Africans would be determined by a comparison between how Britain and Africans would have fared in this imagined world and how they fared in the actual world. If Britain had not exploited Africans then it might have declined in wealth and power to the detriment of present British people. But it had other sources of trade and other countries to exploit, and a failure to exploit Africans might have had little or no effect on the present well-being of British people. If Britain had not exploited Africa then perhaps Africans would now be better off. But it is all too likely that other European powers would have expanded their own trade in slaves and colonised Africa, leaving the condition of Africans no better than it is in the real world. Why then should we suppose that Britain owes reparation to Africa?

The problem lies in the frame of reference. The fact that Britain had other sources of wealth and the high probability that other European countries would have caused as much harm should not invalidate a reparative claim against a nation that *did* exploit Africans. Daniel Butt (2012) argues that we should determine reparative debt by reference to a contrary-to-fact world in which European (and Arab) nations always dealt justly with Africans. What Britain owes in reparation is determined by the difference between how the British and the Africans would have fared in this ideal world and how they fare in the actual world. Butt thinks that the reparative debt of former enslaving and colonial powers, so calculated, is bound to be substantial.

However, nations do not exist in a just world. In a just world no nation would be disadvantaged by not participating in an injustice. In the actual world, refusal to do wrong can be disastrous. Suppose that Britain's economy in the actual world, perhaps its very survival, depended on trading slaves or acquiring colonies. Is it fair to make it pay reparation for what it did by necessity?

To suppose that Britain was compelled to trade slaves is implausible, given that it acted unilaterally to end the trade. The fact that Parliament debated the issue for twenty years before voting for abolition indicates that many people regarded abolition as a viable option at an earlier time. Britain's imperial acquisitions were also heavily criticised by people who thought that the country would do better without them. But even if we suppose that its economic prosperity and political survival depended on exploiting Africa, this does not cancel its reparative responsibility. Britain shares outcome responsibility for whatever harms it caused to Africans. It benefited from injustice. Since this injustice was committed jointly by European and Arab countries, it would be appropriate if they acted together to make reparation. But even if coordinated action is unlikely, Britain, as a beneficiary of injustice, has a reparative obligation.

If Europeans had dealt justly with Africans they would not have engaged in the slave trade. They would have confined themselves to other forms of trade. Perhaps Africans would have become migrant workers in the cane and cotton fields of the New World. Their greater immunity to tropical diseases would have made them in demand as workers in the Caribbean and many other places. We can suppose that they would have behaved and fared much like migrant workers of today. They would have sent money and other goods back to their families, making their communities more prosperous. Some would have paid for their families to join them but many more would eventually have returned home bringing with them savings, skills and new ideas. As the result of trade, increasing wealth and spread of knowledge, Africans would have shared in the developments that led to the creation of modern societies.

In this just world, people of African communities would not only acquire wealth produced by trading their resources and selling their labour. They would also, through investment of capital earned by trade and labour and through the spread of ideas, share the wealth produced by the use of their resources and by the industries that used their labour. Let us assume that their nations would now enjoy prosperity comparable to the prosperity of Western nations. Should we conclude that Britain's reparative debt is the difference between its present GNP and the present GNP of the nations in the territories it exploited?

To reach this conclusion we have to assume that Africans in the just world would have taken the same path to industrialisation and modernity as the Europeans – despite differences in culture and political organisation. The problem with making this assumption is not only that it might be false. It also fails to allow for the fact that benefits and losses are the result of many factors including the choices of individuals and societies. A calculation of debt that assumes that Britain should surrender all it gained by having a history that includes slave trading and colonialism is mistaken. Even if the capital that financed Britain's industrial revolution came from the slave trade, as some people think, it is wrong to regard all the wealth created by this revolution as unjust enrichment. These benefits also owed their existence to the work and skills of the British people and their economic and political relationships. Nor can all the present disadvantages of Africans be blamed on the injustice of Europeans. Africans contributed to the making of their own history.

To calculate Britain's reparative debt we need to know what counts as unjust enrichment. This description is correctly used when people acquire an asset or resource that rightly belongs to others, profit from an investment in this resource, or when they participate in the commission of an injustice – as did plantation owners in Haiti and those who invested in its system of slavery. It is also rightly applied when people receive benefits from an injustice as a gift or inheritance. But the description is not rightly applied to wealth created from the fruits of injustice by people who did not participate in the wrong. The wealth that the British obtained from participating in or supporting the slave trade was unjust enrichment, but not all the gains by workers or investors in industries that were founded on capital acquired through the slave trade or all the money made by manufacturers who used the products of slavery as their raw material.

However, if British ships had provided transport only for Africans going to the New World as free workers or had been forced to find other trade that did not involve supplying slaves, then the profits of ship owners would have been lower. If the British had paid a fair price for the labour and other resources of Africans, then costs to British plantation owners, merchants, manufacturers and consumers would have been higher. The difference between what these people gained in the actual world from exploitation of Africans and what they would have received in the just world counts as unjust enrichment. These gains trickled down to their crews, workers, customers and all others who had dealings with them. They were incorporated into the British economy and shared by all British citizens. The value of these benefits increased as the British economy prospered, just as an invested sum of money increases as interest is accrued, thus providing increasing enrichment to subsequent generations.

How do we calculate the amount of this unjust enrichment? The estimate is bound to be rough and to depend on a lot of assumptions. But if these assumptions are plausible we can reach a conclusion about what Britain owes that is good enough to function as a guideline in negotiations about reparation. First, we need an estimate of wealth gained by slave traders and by industries that directly serviced the slave trade. Records of profits made by slave traders, cotton manufacturers and other companies that supplied equipment or goods for the slave trade can provide a basis for this estimate. Given the assumption that most of this wealth was incorporated into the British economy, we can estimate what present citizens have gained from slavery by calculating what would have been added to this amount if it had been invested, say, in government bonds.

What Britain owes in reparation depends on a comparison between the actual world and how the British and Africans would have fared in the just world. Let us make the reasonable assumption that British ships in that world transported Africans to work as free labourers and that Africans with their increasing wealth bought British goods, including cotton cloths. Plantation owners and perhaps Africans themselves would have paid for the voyages. We can get an idea of how much ship owners would profit by records of travel fees paid by free immigrants and by the demand for plantation labour. We can use records of sales to domestic and foreign markets and estimates of costs that would have been added to prices of raw materials by paid (rather than slave) labour to estimate how British manufacturers would have fared in an economy without slavery and the slave trade. We can assume that their profits, like the wealth of the slave trade, would have been incorporated into the British economy and passed down through the generations. Unjust enrichment gained by the British from the slave trade thus equals the amount gained in the real world minus the amount that they would have acquired in a reckoning of profit and loss for their industries in the just world. Calculation would be difficult, much would be guesswork and the results would be controversial, but they would be good enough to give us a rough idea of what Britain gained from slavery and the slave trade.

However, the case for reparation to Africa depends not only on the continued possession by the British of benefits from the slave trade. It also depends on Africans being excluded, generation after generation, from sharing the wealth gained from this injustice.

Some apparent benefits to Africans should not be counted. African chiefs and their communities profited from trading slaves. But benefits handed over by British agents in pursuit of an injustice do not diminish their reparative debt. In any case, the slave trade was not beneficial for most Africans – in the long run not even for those who traded slaves.

However, Britain did provide benefits to Africans after it abolished the slave trade by patrolling the African coast to intercept slaving vessels, burning down fortresses where slaves were kept and putting pressure on other countries to stop trading slaves. It set up a colony in Africa for the Africans freed from slave ships and it attempted to provide African communities with alternative sources of income. Later when Britain established colonies in Africa it built roads, railways, mines, factories and schools. It established legal and political institutions that most African nations continue to use. It continues to provide assistance to Africa. Nigeria, once a hunting and shipping ground for slaves and a former colony of Britain, is one of the top recipients of British foreign aid. Do the benefits it has supplied to Africa since the days of the slave trade reduce – perhaps even eliminate – its reparative debt?

Though its efforts in the nineteenth century to stop the slave trade may have had more to do with international rivalries than a desire to benefit Africans, Britain deserves credit for acting justly. However, its just actions do not relieve its reparative debt. Those who commit or contribute to an injustice have two moral obligations. The first is to stop doing wrong. They may also have an obligation to stop others from doing wrong if they are capable of doing so without incurring unbearable costs. The second obligation is to make reparation to their former victims. Fulfilling the first obligation does not eliminate or lessen the second. The same reply can be made to those who argue that the cost of fighting the Civil War eliminated the reparative obligation of the United States government to former slaves. The Civil War brought about the end of an injustice, but the victims of slavery were nevertheless entitled to reparation.

The reparative actions that the British did undertake were not effective and may have done more harm than good to Africans by paving the way for colonialism. If the infrastructure and institutions built by the British in their African colonies were designed to further their ability to exploit and control Africans, then their value does not ease the reparative debt of the British any more than the value of the former slave plantations in Haiti erases the reparative debt of the French. The fact that Africans later found a use for them is irrelevant.

Let us assume, however, that some of this infrastructure was built to benefit Africans or, more plausibly, that this was one motivation for building it. We do not know what Africans would have done in the just world but we can assume that they would have been in a better position to build infrastructure and institutions suitable to their needs and traditions. They would have been in a better position to do the work of modernising their societies. The exploitation of Africa for slaves and resources prevented them from being in this position. It would be unfair to allow the British to subtract from their reparations bill the present value of all that they built in Africa.

However, the British did supply materials and expertise to modernise Africa, something they might have done in the just world, and it is reasonable to subtract the value of these contributions from their reparative obligations – given that Africans have really benefited. To roughly calculate this sum we can refer to records of the cost of supplying materials used for construction of infrastructure and the cost of paying and supporting engineers, administrators and other relevant experts, and then adjust this sum to reflect present values. But if the British are justified in claiming credit for building African infrastructure they must also add to their reparative debt the enrichment gained from the resources that they extracted from their African colonies. The aid that Britain now gives to African countries may count toward meeting its reparative obligations, depending on its purpose, but it is not likely to reduce significantly a debt that, as Butt suggests, is likely to be considerable.

Some African nations are badly governed. Some are ruled by dictators. Corruption is rife in many of these countries. Reparation payments might line the pockets of the rulers or enable them to purchase military equipment to conduct wars and suppress their population. This is not a reason for a refusal to pay any reparations to Africa. Not all governments are oppressive or corrupt. Most countries have some form of democracy, and European nations should not be quick to make paternalistic judgement about desert. There can be reasons to hold reparation payments in trust when it is clear that they would be misappropriated or used to suppress the population. But for the most part it is up to Africans to determine how they will be governed and how they will use wealth that is rightly theirs.

Reparation for Slavery in the United States

The best reason for reparation for slavery in the United States is the harm visited on descendants of slaves and other black Americans by a history of injustices rooted in slavery. In a just world Africans would never have been taken from their communities to work as slaves in the tobacco and cotton fields of the South or they would have come voluntarily as paid labourers. But an appeal to what would have been the case in a just world is no help in determining what is owed to American blacks as reparation for an unjust history.

If Africans had never been taken from their homelands then their present descendants would mostly be living in Africa and would have the interests and aspirations of people of their culture. But the descendants of slaves are Americans by birth and culture. They have interests that reflect their position in American society. A comparison between the situation of people in the imagined African world and African Americans not only requires a lot of speculation about how Africans would have fared in the absence of the slave trade; it is also not relevant to the present interests and social environment of African Americans.

Suppose that Africans had come to America as paid labourers and that they and their descendants had always been justly treated. Many of these labourers would have eventually returned to their African communities. Some of those who stayed might have established communities where they could continue to practise their culture and pass it on to their descendants. Others might have been assimilated, perhaps in time becoming indistinguishable from other Americans. In one way or another the lives of the descendants of these free labourers would be so different from the lives of present black Americans as to make a comparison between the just world and the real world irrelevant for the purposes of reparation.

Let us focus instead on what advocates of reparation to former slaves were trying to accomplish. The third principle of reparative justice says that harm done to victims by an injustice should be undone. But much of the harm done by slavery could not be undone. Slaves could not be taken back to the communities from which they or their ancestors were taken. Even if that were possible it would not have suited the majority of former slaves, who had been born in America and had no contact with the African communities from which their ancestors came. The best that could have been done to undo the harm of the injustice was to make it possible for former slaves to have a good life as free citizens in their present society. Since America was supposed to offer civil rights, protection of law and equal opportunity to all of its citizens this meant extending these rights, protections and opportunities to former slaves. Since slavery left its victims destitute and often without the education or resources needed to take advantage of citizenship, appropriate reparation would have also made up for this lack.

Stevens' reparation bill, I suggested, is best interpreted as an attempt to provide former slaves with the resources to make a new life as American citizens. Whether the bill offered sufficient compensation for the harm of slavery is debatable. In any case, reparation was not made and further injustices were done to former slaves and their descendants. Reparative responsibility for the harm done by this history of injustice was passed down to succeeding generations of American citizens. The objective remained the same – to undo the harm, so far as possible, by providing victims of an unjust history with the ability to flourish as free and equal American citizens. But the measures required to achieve this objective changed with changing conditions. Let us assume that land for farming and agricultural equipment, along with preparation for the responsibilities of ownership would have provided former slaves with the resources that they needed to prosper as free Americans. But when America became an industrial nation and when many black Americans became factory or service workers and faced new forms of injustice, other kinds of compensation would have better answered to their needs.

What is now owed in reparation to black Americans are measures to overcome the harms resulting from a history of injustice that began with slavery. There are, as we have seen, three kinds of harm that can be identified as the consequences of this history. First, there are the lingering effects of racism embedded in American institutions that prevent African Americans from being respected and treated as equal citizens. Second, there are the psychological harms that come from past and present injustices: alienation, a low sense of self-worth and lack of hope for the future. Third, there are the intergenerational disadvantages that result from policies that excluded black Americans from benefits, grants and protections provided by governments to white citizens.

What policies should be adopted to overcome these harms can only be settled by consultation with black citizens and available evidence about what is effective in overcoming discrimination and inequality. A presidential apology and efforts to include a black perspective in official histories are obvious ways of addressing psychological harms, but they are not sufficient. More money spent on schools and public services in communities where black Americans live are ways of overcoming the intergenerational harm that results from past government policies and officially tolerated discriminatory practices. But other programmes are likely to be necessary to overcome the attitudes and disadvantages that have reproduced themselves through the generations and to compensate those who have been victims of discrimination. Revival of affirmative action policies may provide more opportunities to some black citizens, but it might be more effective to provide young African Americans with grants for education and training and payments to those who cannot take advantage of these programmes. Persisting effects of historical injustices are likely to be difficult to overcome and may require many different strategies over a long period of time (Spinner-Halev 2012). One of the most urgent requirements is to combat the racism that remains endemic in American society.

If reparation is conceived as compensation for disadvantages resulting from a history of injustice then how does it differ from forward-looking attempts to bring about a more just society? This question revives the debate about the respective roles of reparative and distributive justice. I argued that those who think we should concentrate exclusively on the forward-looking task of making society more just are mistaken. Reparative justice answers to the interests of those who suffer the psychological and material effects of a history of injustice. But if reparative measures turn out to be exactly the same as reforms with forward-looking aims, then why should we care whether they are championed by proponents of reparation or proponents of distributive justice?

Proposals for reform advocated from the perspective of reparative justice are not identical to proposals advocated by proponents of distributive justice. Apology and other kinds of acknowledgement of wrong play an essential role in reparation. They cannot be dispensed with. But even if we ignore this important difference between reparation and justice that is merely forward-looking, there are likely to be differences that result from the considerations that motivate reparation. If the aim is simply to make a society more just for present and future generations, then the most effective programmes are likely to be those that emphasise assistance to young people. Supporters of reparation will also aim to open up opportunities for the young and future generations. But they will be equally concerned to compensate those who have suffered all their lives from the consequences of an unjust history.

Suppose, however, that social programmes to make society more just for black Americans and programmes to satisfy the requirements of reparative justice turn out to be exactly the same. This would not make either perspective redundant. Having more than one reason for a reform is likely to increase support for it. Moreover, the fact that some citizens have an entitlement to reparation gives them a priority that is not shared by all of those who suffer disadvantage. A nation ought to pay its reparative debts. This moral requirement should be satisfied before it decides how to distribute the remainder of its resources. Black Americans, to be sure, are not the only citizens who suffer from the consequences of an unjust history, and negotiation and compromise are likely to be necessary to reach a settlement that is fair to all who are victims of an unjust history and not unfair to those who have to pay.

The reparative debt falls on all taxpaying citizens, including more prosperous black Americans. But this situation is neither paradoxical nor unusual.

Any taxpayer who receives benefits from their government is helping to pay for them. Nor is it unfair. Priority must be given to those who have suffered most from the unjust history and they are more likely to be black Americans who are not so well off.

Reparation to African Americans as I have defended it is compensation for opportunities lost and injuries suffered as the result of an unjust history rooted in slavery. It does not require that all the benefits that white Americans have obtained as the result of slavery be surrendered. However, if compensation to African Americans enables them to overcome the disadvantages of a history of injustice rooted in slavery then they will be in the position to obtain a much greater share of the benefits of their society. Reparation does not require that black Americans receive what they would have got if their ancestors had been justly treated. This idea of reparative justice, as we have seen, is impossible to apply. What they are owed is the reparation that was denied to their ancestors – the basis for enjoying all the rights and opportunities that their society is supposed to make available to its citizens.

Conclusion: The Future of Reparation

In recent times, nations have acknowledged and made reparation for some of their historical wrongs. In 2013 Great Britain apologised and paid reparation to Kenyans tortured by British forces during the Mau Mau rebellion in the 1950s. In 1988 the US government paid reparation to Japanese-Americans interned during World War II. However, the monumental injustices of modern times – the ones that most affected the history of nations and the fate of individuals and families – have been largely unaddressed. Slavery is the most prominent example.

One of the reasons for this failure is the belief that historical injustices like slavery are outside the scope of reparative justice because all of its victims and perpetrators are dead. In this book I have explained why some reparative entitlements and obligations persist through the generations. Among them are entitlements to reparation for slavery and the slave trade.

Another reason why leaders and citizens resist the idea that reparation is owed for slavery is because they suspect that the cost will be considerable – especially if the debt for colonisation of Africa is added to the bill. The prospect is made more unpalatable by the fear that agreeing to make reparation for slavery would create a precedent for further demands. History is full of injustices.

Reparation can be paid over a long period of time. Payments might involve waiving of debts owed to financial institutions by African or Caribbean countries or transfers of technology and expertise. Conflicts between moral requirements and political feasibility can often be resolved through compromise. Most African and Caribbean leaders who demand reparation for slavery are not asking for large sums of money but rather for more assistance in providing their populations with better services.

Michael Walzer (1983) argues that historical connections between peoples or nations create special obligations. Slavery and the slave trade created such connections between Europeans and Africans and between American governments and their black citizens. The first step toward fulfilling these obligations is to acknowledge that they exist. The form reparation actually takes will be determined by negotiation, legal precedents, political considerations and moral argument. This book focuses on the moral considerations. The practical task of making reparation is an undertaking for the future.

Bibliography

Acharya, A., Blackwell, M. and Sen, M. (2016). The Political Legacy of American Slavery. *The Journal of Politics* 78(3), pp. 621–41.

Amighetti, S. and Nuti, A. (2015). Towards a Shared Redress: Achieving Historical Justice through Democratic Deliberation. *Journal of Political Philosophy*, 23(4), pp. 385–405.

Aristotle. *Nicomachean Ethics*, Vol. 4(4). [Any Edition]

Babacar, M. (2006). The Economic, Political, and Social Impact of the Atlantic Slave Trade on Africa. *The European Legacy: Toward New Paradigms*, 11(6), pp. 607–62.

Barkan, E. (2000). *The Guilt of Nations: Restitution and Negotiating Historical Injustices*. New York, London: W.W. Norton and Company.

Bittker, B. (1973). *The Case for Black Reparations*. New York: Random House.

Boxill, B. (2003). A Lockean Argument for Black Reparations. *The Journal of Ethics*, 7(1), pp. 63–91.

Butt, D. (2012). Repairing Historical Wrongs and the End of Empire. *Social and Legal Studies* 21(2), pp. 227–42.

Butt, D. (2008). *Rectifying International Injustice*. Oxford: Oxford University Press.

Butt, D. (2006). Nations, Overlapping Generations and Historic Injustice. *American Philosophical Quarterly*, 43(4), pp. 357–67.

Coates, T. (2014). The Case for Reparations. *The Atlantic*, https://www.theatlantic.com/magazine/archive/2014/06/the-case-for-reparations/361631 (Accessed 30 May 2017).

Craemer, T. (2015). Estimating Slavery Reparations: Present Value Comparisons of Historical Multigenerational Reparations Policies. *Social Science Quarterly*, 96(2), pp. 639–55.

Dubois, L. (2004). *Avengers of the New World: The Story of the Haitian Revolution*. Cambridge, MA: Belknap Press.

Dunn, R. (1972). *Sugar & Slaves: The Rise of the Planter Class in the English West Indies, 1624–1713*. Chapel Hill, NC: University of North Carolina Press.

Fullinwider, R. (2002). Preferential Hiring and Compensation. In: S. Cahn, ed., *The Affirmative Action Debate*. New York: Routledge, pp. 68–78.

Fullinwider, R. (2000). The Case for Reparations. *Philosophy and Public Policy Quarterly*, 20(2/3), pp. 1–8, https://philpapers.org/archive/FULTCF-2.pdf (Accessed 20 September 2017).

Hare, R.M. (1979). What is Wrong with Slavery? *Philosophy and Public Affairs*, 8(2), pp. 103–21.

Henry, C.P. (2003). The Politics of Racial Reparations. *Journal of Black Studies*, 34(2), pp. 131–52.

Howard-Hassmann, R.E. (2003). Moral Integrity and Reparations for Africa. In: J. Torpey, ed., *Politics and the Past: On Repairing Historical Injustices*. Lanham, Maryland: Rowman and Littlefield, pp. 193–211.

List, C. and Pettit, P. (2011). *Group Agency: The Possibility, Design and Status of Corporate Agents*. Oxford and New York: Oxford University Press.

McCarthy, T. (2004). Coming to Terms with Our Past, Part II: On the Morality and Politics of Reparations for Slavery. *Political Theory*, 32(6), pp. 750–72.

McCarthy, T. (2002). On the Politics and Memory of Slavery. *Political Theory*, 30(5), pp. 623–48.

Meyer, L. (2006). Reparations and Symbolic Restitution. *Journal of Social Philosophy*, 37(3), pp. 406–22.

Miller. D. (2007). *National Responsibility and Global Justice*. Oxford and New York: Oxford University Press.

Nozick, R. (1974). *Anarchy, State and Utopia*. New York: Basic Books.

Pew Research Centre (2016). On Views of Race and Inequality, Blacks and Whites Are Worlds Apart, http://assets.pewresearch.org/wp-content/uploads/sites/3/2016/06/ST_2016.06.27_Race-Inequality-Final.pdf (Accessed 20 September 2017).

Pierik, R. (2006). Reparations for Luck Egalitarians. *Journal of Social Philosophy*, 37(3), pp. 423–40.

Pogge, T. (2002). *World Poverty and Human Rights*. Cambridge: Polity.

Robinson, R. (2000). *The Debt: What America Owes to Blacks*. New York: Penguin.

Salzberger, R. and Tuck, M. (2004). *Reparations for Slavery: A Reader*. Lanham, Maryland: Rowman and Littlefield.

Sher, G. (1981). Ancient Wrongs and Modern Rights. *Philosophy and Public Affairs*, 10(1), pp. 3–17.

Spinner-Halev, J. (2012). *Enduring Injustice*. Cambridge: Cambridge University Press.

Thomas, H. (1997). *The Slave Trade: The Story of the Atlantic Slave Trade 1440–1870*. New York: Simon and Schuster.

Thompson, J. (2002). *Taking Responsibility for the Past: Reparation and Historical Injustice*. Cambridge: Polity.

Vernon, R. (2012). *Historical Redress: Must We Pay For the Past?* London: Continuum.

Vernon, R. (2003). Against Restitution. *Political Studies*, 51(3), pp. 542–57.

Waldron, J. (1992). Superseding Historic Injustice. *Ethics*, 103(1), pp. 4–28.

Walker, M.U. (2010). Truth Telling as Reparations. *Metaphilosophy*, 41(4), pp. 525–45.

Walzer, M. (1983). *Spheres of Justice: A Defense of Pluralism and Equality*. New York: Basic Books.

Wenar, L. (2006), Reparations for the Future. *Journal of Social Philosophy*, 37(4), pp. 377–405.

Winter, S. (2006). Uncertain Justice: History and Reparations. *Journal of Social Philosophy*, 37(3), pp. 342–59.

Young, I.M. (2006). Responsibility and Global Justice: A Social Connection Model. *Social Philosophy and Policy*, 23(1), pp. 102–30.